# GLIMPSES OF TRUTH

# GLIMPSES OF TRUTH

WITH ESSAYS ON

***EPICTETUS AND MARCUS AURELIUS***

**RT. REV. J. L. SPALDING**

GYAN

*Published by*

Gyan Publishing House
5, Ansari Road
Daryaganj, New Delhi-110002
Phone: 011-47034999, 9811692060
E-mail: books@gyanbooks.com

*Distribution Network*
gyanbooks.com
India, USA, Canada, UK, Australia, France



ISBN : 978-81-212-9628-1 (PB)
First Published, 1903

2nd Impression 2023

*Printed at:* Gyan Press, Delhi.



**GLIMPSES OF TRUTH**
Author: RT. REV. J. L. SPALDING

A.W. Elson & Co. Boston
J L Spalding
Bp of Peoria.

# Glimpses of Truth

WITH ESSAYS ON

*EPICTETUS AND MARCUS AURELIUS*

BY

RT. REV. J. L. SPALDING

Bishop of Peoria

1903

# CONTENTS

# GLIMPSES OF TRUTH

EVERY surmise and vaticination of the mind is entitled to a certain respect, and we learn to prefer imperfect theories, and sentences which contain glimpses of truth, to digested systems which have no one valuable suggestion. — EMERSON.

The study of proverbs may be more instructive and comprehensive than the most elaborate scheme of philosophy. — MOTHERWELL.

Good maxims are germs of all good; firmly impressed on the memory they nourish the will. — JOUBERT.

Exclusively of the abstract sciences the largest and worthiest portion of our knowledge consists of aphorisms; and the greatest and best of men is but an aphorism. — COLERIDGE.

Why spin a story when a phrase will tell what thou hast to say? Why read a book when an aphorism will express the truth a volume may hold?

Wisdom becomes current and passes most readily from mind to mind when it is coined into proverbs and maxims, which, holding a world of meaning in small compass, delight by their brevity and stimulate by their wealth of implication. The wise seek these focuses of light and warmth with more eagerness, cling to them with more joy, and cherish them with more devoutness than misers gold.

# GLIMPSES OF TRUTH

## I.

THE delight there is in becoming more and more, whether by acquiring knowledge, or virtue, or insight, or self-control, makes pleasant what else were difficult, tedious, and monotonous. Spiritual growth is the aim and end of life, and nothing that ministers to it can satiate or pall. This makes the happiness of all noble strivers, whether they lay the chief stress on culture of mind, or formation of character, or purification of soul.

How miserable were not those ages in which the writings of Homer and Plato, of Cicero and Virgil, existed, but had fallen into neglect and oblivion. One may or may not deem it a misfortune never to have seen the monuments of Greece and Rome; never to have looked from the Acropolis on the Attic plain and its island-studded sea; never from Taormina's heights to have gazed on the slopes of

Ætna, stooping with their crown of lemon and almond trees and vines to the waters that bathe their feet; but only unraised and sluggish souls, only ignoble and brutish spirits, can consent to die without having drunk the divine words of the greatest and most illumined minds.

The Greek and the Latin, which we call dead languages, are not dead. They cannot die. They live not only in the literatures which they inform and which the world will not suffer to perish, but they enter as a vital force into the tongues of the modern civilized peoples. They inspire, shape, and control the thoughts of the most living minds. They are a spur to the noblest aspirations; they embody the beauty which never grows old; they fire the most generous and gifted of each newborn generation with a courage and an enthusiasm which keep the race fresh and young. They cannot die. They are immortal, because immortal spirits have breathed into them the truth and beauty which are imperishable.

Though thou art in the midst of the world and busy with many things, it is none the less thy duty to live within where the soul finds itself in the company of God and eternal truth; and if this secret be hidden from thee thou art doomed to a superficial and vulgar life. Thou hast not yet attained. To-day thou art reborn. Begin thy life anew. "The greatness or smallness of a man," says Ruskin, "is in the most conclusive sense determined for him at his birth, as strictly as it is determined for a fruit whether it is to be a currant or an apricot. . . . Apricot out of currant — great man out of small, did never yet art or effort make." This is an instance of the readiness with which a comparison may be perverted to insinuate what is false. No sane mind ever imagined that education can develop one species from another, — an eagle from a dove, an apple from a grain of wheat, — and yet Ruskin thinks it necessary to be emphatic in denying what no one affirms. His argument is not merely sophistical, but harmful, tending as it does to take away hope and heart from students and teachers, who are not to labor for anything else than to make the most of what is given them to shape and fashion. Except by ceaseless striving one cannot know what he may become. Each one, certainly, can attain skill in doing whatever he can accustom himself to persevere in doing. Let him learn to occupy himself gladly and unwearyingly with the things of the mind, and he will become wiser and nobler and go farther than as yet he is able to imagine.

The difference between great and small men is not absolute. There are many kinds and degrees of human power and worth; and they who strive faithfully for the best attain it in the measure their talent makes possible. Let the student have boundless trust in the efficacy of self-activity, in the marvellous excellences which the habit of doing patiently and thoroughly is capable of producing in even the most unpromising subjects. Endowments are gifts of nature; but a faculty is not so much developed as produced by education in the large sense of the word. It does more than unfold: it creates, it confers ability to do what without it we should never have power to do. The vital consideration for one who wishes to get an education is whether he have the will and the courage to take infinite pains for years or for a lifetime, and this he cannot have unless he have infinite faith in the supreme worth of a cultivated mind and a perfect character.

However great one's talent or skill, something of it is lost if for a little while, even, he cease to improve himself. This is manifestly true of artists, and it is not less so of those whose instrument is more immediately the mind.

Where man is civilized art prevails over nature, in government, in commerce, in war, in literature, in the professions, in everything. In the progress he has been making for ages he has so transformed his endowments that what he has produced within himself transcends, directs, and controls that which is born in him. Thus a few thousands of a civilized race hold in subjection millions of barbarians. Thus in law, in medicine, and in the ministry, the greatest students, not the greatest talents, reach the summits; and so in literature also they who take endless pains to educate themselves, and not rude genius, write what becomes a permanent part of the spiritual treasures of their people or of mankind. Even in the world of fashion they who are best trained and cultivated, not the best endowed, are the leaders.

In admiring the abilities of others what we really admire is the industry which has produced them, and which would bring forth like faculties in ourselves, had we the will and the courage to become perseveringly self-active. The question of education resolves itself for each one into learning how to learn. Be attentive, observe, inquire, reflect, meditate, compare, weigh, write, not for others, but for your own enlightenment and improvement; and let all this become habitual. The greatest genius, if he would accomplish something worth remembering, must conform to this law; and they who appear to have little talent will, if they obey it faithfully, be found in the end to have much.

Whatever we thoroughly accustom ourselves to becomes pleasant, and often indispensable, however disagreeable it may have been at first. It is this that makes home sweet, country dear, and friends delightful. It is this that gives to study, meditation, and prayer the power to refresh, strengthen, and console.

When the mature look back to their childhood and youth they cannot fail to perceive that most of the things which interested and absorbed them had no value or importance other than that wherewith their ignorance and inexperience endowed them. The toys, the games, the sights and sounds which delighted them they now recognize to have had this power only because they themselves were weak and foolish, the victims of illusion. In the same way a cultivated and reflective mind sees how unworthy of rational beings are the pastimes, pleasures, and ambitions of the many. They too are victims of illusion. If he consider more closely he finds that he also is beguiled by a world of vanities and dreams, that he is but a child of larger growth, whose business, office, reputation, and schemes, if contemplated from the point of view of a higher intelligence, are as insignificant, as ephemeral, as idle as the playthings of children or the amusements and expectations of the ignorant. If all belief in illusion were taken from us life would lose its charm. The estimate each one places on himself is illusive; the importance he ascribes to his thoughts, his words, his works, is fictitious. Were he to perish at once the world would not be more changed than if a mote dropped out of a sunbeam. This is true of the greatest as of the least of mortals. Mankind would be much what they are had their heroes never lived; and what they are, if we view things in the light of eternity, is but as a silly tale. The race is of yesterday and tomorrow it shall have passed away, leaving no trace behind. Unless it is from God, in Him and for Him, it were better it had never been.

If we look at things as they are in themselves, why should we hold that a plant is a higher form of existence than a stone, an animal than a plant, a man than a mere brute? Only faith can supply an adequate answer: faith that mind is superior to matter, that it is more excellent to feel and think, to know and love than simply to exist: and this faith is ineradicably implanted in the human heart. We believe that life is the essential good, that the highest life is the highest form of being, and therefore that the Supreme Being, the primal and creative cause of all that exists, is perfect Life.

Whatever within us is born of strength, whatever awakens a sense of power and vigor, gives pleasure, because we love life and all its potent manifestations. Hence it is delightful to perform deeds of prowess or to see them performed by others. Hence there is a thrill of joy in writing with point and force, in speaking with eloquence and effect, in controlling and guiding the wills of men, in arousing their energies and impelling them to do more than they believed themselves capable of doing; in inspiring faith, hope, and courage; in enkindling the flame of a pure and noble love. There is bliss in reading sublime words, in the exaltation of spirit caused by lofty and impassioned utterances, by deeds of daring, by imposing pageants, by storm and thunderpeal and the ceaseless roar of mighty cataracts; for all this arouses within us a deeper consciousness of the infinite power of life, of the life of Him who breathes in the soul of man and attunes it to harmony with the awful and unimaginable forces which work in endless time and space, and fill the abysmal heavens with light and beauty.

The intelligent even often express surprise that men of great wealth should not be content with what they have, but continue to accumulate. Nothing is less surprising, for whatever man sets his heart on must increase or lose the power to please, whether it be money or knowledge or virtue or fame. To have or to have done can satisfy no one. To feel ourselves alive we must still acquire, still accomplish. Our passions, like our appetites, are never really sated, but only lulled into a repose which prepares them to crave for more. Since our yearning is infinite, let us yearn for the infinite good which is not material, but spiritual; not money and the things it buys, but truth and love, which are above all price.

A chief virtue of vital books lies in their power to reveal us to ourselves, to show us that we possess potentialities of ability of which we were not conscious, and so to stimulate us to effort in the direction of our talents. For many a one the reading of such a book for the first time has been the beginning of a new life. Contact with sublime souls is what is most to be desired, above all for youth. It is capable of producing in them a higher quality of being, of making them something more and better than otherwise they could have become.

The aim and end of education is to produce faculty and ability, and its one method is habituation. To be habituable is the first requirement, the infallible proof of talent. What one can accustom himself to, he can learn to know and do. What is power of attention or observation or reflection but a result of the habit of holding the mind to its objects? The multitude of those who pass through schools fail to become scholars because they fail to acquire the habit of study. He who is habitually attentive, inquiring, observant, eager to learn and to correct his defects, whether of mind or character, whether of thought and speech or of conduct and deportment, necessarily becomes wiser and nobler, whatever difficulties and obstacles confront him. He finds teachers in all that he meets, and in the face of poverty and opposition works his way to a knowledge of men and books.

If we have genuine powers they who throw doubts on our ability stimulate us even more effectually than the expectations and urgency of friends; for real strength, like heroic courage, loves the face of foes.

Creative force secretes itself. It grows in solitude and hiding; craves silence and obscurity; wraps itself in mystery. Where it works the soul bows in awe and holy shame, and from those who live in the glare and noise of the clamorous world, its sacred power departs. There hangs about it the darkness that brooded on primal chaos, from which the Eternal called forth a universe of light and glory. It lies in the seed germinating under ground; it is enfolded in the love of virginal hearts; it moves in the meditations of sincere minds, who in self-forgetfulness and tranquillity bend all their strength to know truth, that they may follow where it leads.

The negative exists for the positive. Rest is for the sake of action. If night buries us in darkness, it is that we may be all alive when day breaks. Silence and solitude are for refreshment of spirit. Continence is for self-control and strength; humility for good sense; abstinence for health. Self-denial is for greater ability to help others, voluntary poverty is for their enrichment; obedience is for the sake of liberty and the common welfare.

Life never seems so short to me as when I think of the books I know something of and should wish to study more and more. I would spend a winter with Plato, another with Dante, another with Shakespeare and Milton, and months or years with the great historians, story-tellers, travellers, and others who can best impart to me what is known of man and nature. Then there is Aristotle, Marcus Aurelius, Epictetus, Montaigne, Descartes, Bacon, Pascal, Wordsworth, Goethe, Emerson, Kant. And when they have all been read and studied, one would wish to begin anew, feeling that now he is able to drink deeper draughts from these perennial fountains of life and joy; for the great books, once we have learned to know and love them, have for us, like the flowers and the stars, unfailing power to touch, to inspire, to console, to strengthen, and to exalt. They are an unending world of wisdom and beauty, and one has but a day to live. When we are in conscious communion with this spiritual infinity and plenitude, we are certain we are immortal.

Since the greater and better part of our happiness is found in the free play of the imagination, when it is inspired by faith, hope, and love; and since the imagination is hindered and confused by the noise of the crowd and by the conversation even of acquaintances and friends, it follows that the purest delight must be sought in solitude, where the soul is unimpeded, and may at will create for itself divine worlds of goodness and beauty. There has never been a great soul whose power was not derived from the communion with God and Nature which solitude makes possible, as it alone refreshes and recreates the wisest and the purest when they have become weary and exhausted. To be near to God is to be in Paradise. Nature too soothes and helps us to dream and meditate; and its fairest scenes would best perform this service were it not that there the idle talk of men never fails to intrude on our bliss.

A man of genius is drawn by the very constitution of his physical and spiritual being to observe, to reflect, to remark, to compare, to give heed to little things, to discover likenesses and dissimilitudes, which escape the notice of ordinary minds. He quickly accustoms himself to his task and readily acquires habits of self-activity. He need not see much to have large experience, nor know much to be able to divine a great deal. A glimpse will show him what full sight fails to reveal to another — a word will lead him to new worlds. He is alive and alert even when he appears to be idle or passive. Something of this power which genius confers on its chosen band the teacher should labor to enable his pupils to acquire; and possibly the best means he can employ is to get them to learn to know and to love the works of men of genius.

The chief value of a man lies in the thought and love his life embodies and reveals, and not in the office he fills or the money he accumulates.

The most marvellous monument of a people's genius is its language; and it is inevitable that the nations which have created the noblest literatures should have formed and polished the most excellent instruments for the expression of their faith and love, their thoughts and emotions. When there is question of a poet or an orator, what we find most admirable in him is the power and perfection of his style. What he says loses some essential quality when it is uttered in other words than his own. His manner is the living vesture of the truth and beauty which he reveals: it is part of the indefinable personal element without which no writing can be literature.

However true and profound one's thoughts may be, he may not hope to introduce them into the circles which are capable of recognizing and appreciating their worth, unless he clothe them in a fitting garb of words, habit them in a style which shall commend and give them currency; and this skill they alone acquire who inure themselves to the labor and fatigue which genuine writing involves. As the musician who aims at excellence lets no day pass without exercise of his talent, so he who would attain beauty, force, and accuracy of verbal expression must keep his pen in hand day by day, and must not weary of subjecting what he writes to his own pitiless criticism, reading, and correcting again and again, still dissatisfied when at last forced to confess that it is the best he can do.

The multitude are busy getting, spending, and procreating; and it is only at rare intervals that one stands aside, and rising above the throng takes as his sole aim, his life-purpose, the focussing and the diffusing of the light of truth, of the glow and fervor of love, — the unsating food which nourishes the soul and sustains faith in humanity. The world, busy getting, spending, and procreating, knows him not or heeds him not. He may live in poverty, he may die in ignominy, and his very name be swallowed in oblivion; but he belongs to the divine breed of men who minister to the spiritual and essential needs of the race, who keep alive on earth the consciousness of eternal right and wrong, who breaking through the prison of the senses rise to the vision of immortal life in and with God.

If the gradual enfeeblement and final extinction of the power to think highly, to resolve nobly, and to love purely were the only curse a base life inflicts, it were none the less more to be dreaded and shunned than poverty, sickness, imprisonment, and the loss of good name and friends. To barter the life of the spirit for the pleasures of sense is to herd with brutes when one might enter the company of the wisest, the fairest, and the holiest.

He who lives not in struggle and combat with himself, if not with others, leads not a human life; for he who does not face and overcome difficulties and obstacles day by day, makes no progress, grows neither in mind nor in character. To this law aggregates not less than individuals are subject. A party or a church which is not opposed becomes corrupt and falls to ruin. Christ shows the way of peace to those who take His cross and contend to the uttermost. He came not, however, to bring peace, but a sword, to inspire the heroic and sublime struggles in which souls athirst for truth, justice, and love confront without fear a world in arms against them. This warfare is the indispensable condition of intellectual, moral, and religious life, and when peace is sought through compromise the result is not peace, but decay and death.

We love the company of those who put us at ease, who entertain and amuse us, who make us self-contented; but only they are helpful to us who stimulate us, who rouse us to effort, who make self-complacent thoughts impossible, who fill us with a yearning for higher things, who inspire a persistent longing to make ourselves wiser, purer, and stronger.

Profound minds compel us to think. In uttering deeper truth than others, they suggest more; and those are frequently the most stimulating whose world view differs from our own. They oblige us to gain a larger comprehension of our position and to grasp with firmer hold the truths which are ours. They persuade us to look again, and help us to more profound intuitions. In following them we grow clear-headed, though abysses yawn and chasms open before our advancing steps, until at length we learn to walk without fear or dread, in a universe which God makes, and makes for those who know and love its truth and beauty. Until we have made ourselves at home in the company of one or several of these supreme minds we are but children for whom the darkness is full of terrors, who people the unknown with imaginary shapes and horrors.

At first view one is tempted to believe that it is the tendency of civilization to make men more alike, since it produces greater uniformity and sameness in customs and manners, in dress and behavior. But the differences among the civilized are deeper and more far-reaching than among savages and barbarians. They are differences of mind and character, of ideas and sentiments. They are radical, they touch the essence of life; while the uncivilized, however dissimilar they may appear to be, are alike in their common ignorance, in their short-sightedness, in their inability to change or make progress in the monotony and dulness of their whole existence. The world they live in is but little removed from that of mere animals. It is a world of appetite and slavish conformity. They look not before and after, but from generation to generation, and from century to century tread the same narrow paths.

"If religion is not true," says Leopardi, "it is man's greatest evil and the supreme injury which his inquiries, reasonings, and meditations, or his illusions, have inflicted upon him." Let us assume that there is no God and no soul, and that religion consequently has no logical or real foundation. The non-existence of God and the soul leaves nothing but the physical universe, and the deepest thought shows that not even that remains in the absence of conscious being. There is no free will, no right nor wrong, no truth nor justice, but man is wholly swallowed in the swirl of matter. If the brief day of earthly life is the beginning and end of human existence, can it be deemed an evil and a supreme injury for man that during the fleeting moments of his passage from nothingness to nothingness he should cherish faith in the freedom of the will, in truth and justice and in the distinction between right and wrong? They alone can think so who, like Leopardi, hold that life itself is a curse.

Old age is a disease to which families and peoples, like individuals, must succumb. Nay, planets and suns, the universe itself, will grow old and perish. To begin to exist is to begin to cease to exist, and brief is whatever comes to end. In this lies the vanity of all things, their shadowlike and unsubstantial nature. It is this that fills the soul with pathos, making it a ghost, haunting a world falling to ruin. It is this that consoles it too, awakening within it the consciousness that though heaven and earth pass away, it, like God, shall endure. My childhood and youth yielded to time and vanished; the friends that sprang about me as flowers bloom in the spring, faded and fell. Again and again my garden has become a wilderness, but I myself survive, and shall though a thousand homes should harbor me and then turn to charnel-houses.

For trouble and misfortune we may find some consolation in reflecting that they are generally less real and grave than imagination would lead us to believe, and that if rightly borne they are rarely without a remedy or some resulting good. When we look back we are aware that the cares and sorrows which threatened to overwhelm us passed away without inflicting fatal injury, but not without leaving us gentler and wiser. So it may be with all the evils which can befall if we are but true. The only ills in which no good can be found are a mind debased, a conscience deadened, a soul which sin has made incapable of faith, hope, and love.

The more religious and the more philosophic the mind, the less one feels the need of associating his life and happiness with any other than God; and this growing isolation from the things and beings that are passing away does not diminish love and sympathy and the desire to be of help, but gives them a purer quality and a deeper efficacy.

Consciousness of defects is largely wanting. The near-sighted believe they see as well as others until experiment forces them to recognize their shortness of vision. They who have no ear for music are not aware of the fact unless it is forced on their attention; nor do those who lack the sense for beauty feel the deficiency. The miser and the lecher think all men are like themselves. It does not occur to the savage or the barbarian to imagine that his language is but a jargon. The things to which we are accustomed appear to be good enough until we have been made acquainted with better. The old ways satisfy us so long as we have no knowledge of the new; and hence a change from a lower to a higher environment arouses dormant energies and brings wider worlds into view. It is the purpose of education to enable us to perceive wherein we are lacking and to awaken within us an ever-growing desire to overcome the defects of which the educative process makes us conscious. The result is the self-activity which is the condition and the secret of progress, intellectual, moral, æsthetic, and religious.

We find what we seek if the seeking be persistent, and what we crave be wisdom and righteousness, purity and peace.

Become and do the best it is possible for thee to become and do, and it matters not at all by what title thou art known, or how environed and attended. In what bodily form the soul may have dwelt, or in the midst of what circumstances, is insignificant. All this fades and melts to nothingness. But the divine thought, the heroic temper, the undying hope, are imperishable and forever precious. Greatness of soul alone, says Pericles, never grows old.

The crowd will never believe that position and wealth are doubtful goods; but the wisest and the purest know that whatever draws the soul to the surface and binds it in servitude to matter is a hindrance to the truest and highest life.

We truly pray only for what we persistently work for.

We can beseech God to give us only what we desire, admire, long for, believe in, and feel the need of. It is easy therefore to pray for health and wealth, but our hearts and words grow faint when we ask our Father in heaven to make us lowly-minded and pure, unselfish and loving, obedient and resigned.

Youth intoxicates, and lust and greed and hate and ambition; and it is as hard to find a sober man as a true man.

In politics or war an accident may make one famous; but they whom wisdom and virtue make known live in worlds where chance has no meaning.

In moments of the highest spiritual exaltation the forms of time and space fall from the soul, and man feels himself alive in the light of God's eternal, absolute being.

He is rich who is able and willing to impart to whomsoever he meets the best wealth — truth and wisdom and whatever else is spiritual power.

To know the best that has been done and said profits little, unless we love and live by it all, replunging day by day into the sweet and purifying stream.

We can never be thankful enough that there is always good work to do.

True insight is the rarest of gifts — the distinctive mark of sanctity and genius.

The essential goods are good thoughts, good desires, good deeds. That they may be, the universe exists.

The ideal is not pleasure, but virtue and power. "Life," says Marcus Aurelius, "is more like wrestling than dancing."

As a man's appetites assert themselves despite all obstacles, so his religion, if it be more than a name, will have irresistible sway over him.

The general tenor of life is the same for all, and superior natures are revealed by their ability to make occasional escapes into the higher world of thought and love. The commonplace pursues us everywhere, and the greatest minds even are driven to utter themselves, except in fortunate moments, in the commonplace.

Where there is true worth there will be appreciation, if not immediately, in the end. But they who are eager to be recognized can neither say nor do aught on which the mark of permanent value can be stamped.

The deeper and more real our knowledge the more wonderful we perceive the objects of thought to be; and so the wise come to understand that the beatitude of the All-perfect can be nothing else than self-contemplation — the highest form of self-activity wherein the antithesis between subject and object is transcended and subsumed.

My faith, hope, love, knowledge, interest, in whatever thing or cause, are determined chiefly by what I myself am. In mere matter there is no faith, hope, love, knowledge, or interest of whatever kind; and the higher we ascend in the scale of being, the higher our faith, hope, love, knowledge, and interest become.

Whether it be due to youth and immaturity, or to ignorance and stupidity, or to uncontrolled animal instinct and perversity, there are innumerable human beings who become the more enslaved and worthless the more they are given freedom to do as they please.

There is an all-pervading transubstantiation of nature into spiritual realities. The waves of sound set in motion by the voice are, as they strike on the ear, but atmospheric vibrations which the soul transmutes into symbols of truth, goodness, and beauty. In the laws of nature mind utters itself to mind. That which is borne in upon us from without is akin to us; it has significance and value for us; it is a message from the Eternal to beings whom He has called into existence that they may become and know and love more and more for ever and ever. Except for souls by whom it is seen, known, and loved there can be no beauty nor truth nor goodness.

The beautiful is useful also, its highest use lying in its power to lift man to worlds where he may see within, above, and beyond all that appears, the infinite wisdom and love of God.

Whatever is is a result of the nature of things and is by God's permission. Let nothing then disturb thee or weaken thy efforts to become obedient, just, loving, and serviceable.

Self-respect is an essential good. Where it is lacking, nothing by which life may be environed can give true contentment or delight, while whatever heightens it brings joy. Since right conduct is the chief nourisher of self-respect, a virtuous life is the happiest.

Good name environs and commends a man like a beautiful home, or a becoming dress, or the company of the gracious and refined. It is, the scripture says, a sweet-smelling unguent.

Of many of the minor virtues on which happiness and success so largely depend, we may say that to acquire them it is sufficient not to despise them.

The things we believe in, admire, and desire genuinely and perseveringly are at length inwrought into the substance of our being. "As a man thinketh in his heart, so is he." *Abeunt studia in mores.*

Custom rules the world more than opinion, for opinion is born of custom.

Laws which are not supported and enforced by public opinion are ineffectual, because laws are little else than the authoritative expression and proclamation of public opinion.

Rights imply duties and are measured by them. One has the right to do what duty commands, and in the strict sense no other right. The higher and holier the duties the more sacred and inviolable the rights. The wise and the good lay claim to no right but to be of service, desire no freedom but to obey conscience.

If thou canst but grow wise and loving enough, men will clamor for thy help as the famishing cry for food.

No thoughts, hopes, beliefs, aims, or deeds are good unless, if known to others, they inspire courage and sympathy and consequently aversion from whatever is hurtful to human life.

As mightiest men have found more comfort in the love of some poor woman than in the worship of the world, so the wisest cherish simple truth more than all wealth and fame.

Life is the supreme good. Teach me, O heavenly Father, to know and love more and more the truth which shall compel me to live the life which is Thyself; for I can rightly know divine truth and beauty and goodness only in so far as my believing, yearning, and striving incorporate them in my life.

Truth is formal and cold unless emotion clothe it with warmth and evoke its vital power. They who have best wrought this miracle have most surely escaped oblivion; for they have touched the secret spring of the most imperishable and the most irresistible thing in man, which is sentiment; and so long as their words shall survive, so long shall that which is deepest and most enduring in our nature respond to their appeal.

Let those whose life is on the surface have position and wealth; but live thou within where the soul makes itself a home.

The cause which makes the universe a cosmos must be, in its inmost nature, intelligent and moral. This is a truth of reason; but I need it not, for a thousand times God has saved me from my ignorance, blindness, and folly, reaching forth as from the inner heart of being a hand of guidance and love.

One who leads the life which reason and conscience reveal and prescribe feels the unsatisfactoriness of whatever is external, whether it be some object in nature or the artificial world in which ambition, greed, and sensuality are the ruling forces. He gets insight into the fact that in the beginning, midmost, and in the end, the soul, with its abiding universe of truth, goodness, and beauty, is the primal and ultimate reality and value. He understands therefore that if a man lose his soul, — his faith, his hope, his aspiration and his love, — all gain is loss.

And so, says Socrates, as Plato reports in Gorgias, bidding farewell to those things which most men account honors, and looking forward to the truth, I shall earnestly endeavor to grow so far as may be in goodness, and thus live, and thus, when the time comes, die.

The ground of my confidence, the joy I find in believing in God and in His Christ, is enrooted in the hope that I may still improve; for if I could be certain that I should never become wiser or more unselfish or more loving I should despair and feel there is no God. Since, then, my capacity for self-improvement is the mainspring of my happiness, I am senseless if I do not strive day by day to grow better, more reverent, more self-devoted, more lowly-minded, more loving.

They who keep climbing will at last find themselves alone where nothing but God's presence has power to cheer and console. Shall we therefore prefer the low levels where men beguile and delude themselves with the chasing of phantoms?

If like God man could know all things, like Him he would have all power, for knowledge is the highest form of power; and since to grow like to God is his one business, it is his duty to seek wisdom and understanding not less than purity and righteousness.

The divine discontent, while it leaves us strength and will to do the best we can do, drives us so to perform the task that our work shall become an encouragement to many and a light to the yet unborn; so to act that what we do may not only be in harmony with the eternal laws, but may possess also something of the charm which nothing but a noble personality can give to words and deeds.

To lose faith in God is to abandon hope; for however much we laud our prosperities, we know and feel that unless God is, it is all but a comedy of fools and a dance of death. If we cannot lay hold on Him we are aware, even in the midst of those who trust and love us, that we are but decoys to lure to nothingness; useless even for this, since the inevitable end is the extinction of all consciousness. Our ever-widening knowledge of nature and history involves us in intellectual and moral difficulties which may be insuperable; but if we could be certain that the universe is self-evolved, and that the fatal process is from the unconscious to the unconscious, all seriousness, all speech of law and right and duty would be as ridiculous as the clutter of apes.

If thou wouldst accomplish something of worth, think not of thyself but of thy work.

To be a true and unfailing helper and benefactor one must have ceased to care whether the good he does shall ever be known, or if known whether credit shall be given to him. He must be of service as unselfishly as the flowers bloom and the light diffuses itself, as the waters leap and the birds sing; and his reward must be the consciousness of doing right, which is the unfailing source of life and joy.

The abidingly interesting and attractive are made so, not by their physical but by their intellectual and moral qualities. The most beautiful woman if she be dull or ignorant or coarse or shrewish quickly loses the power to please and becomes an object of indifference or repulsion.

The man of action must throw himself into the full stream of life; but the thinker if he is to think to good purpose must withdraw from the turmoil of the world.

The wise think of the virtues more than of the vices of men; for the good inspire hope and confidence, while the example of the wicked, if it do not corrupt, produces at least a certain enfeeblement and despondency.

There is not an atom or a molecule which could have been brought into existence by less than infinite knowledge and power. Within me and without, then, there is infinite knowledge and power. If I am helpless and ignorant, it is because I am hardly alive; and if anything I call mine, as my learning or virtue or property or position, is a good for me, it is so only in so far as it makes me more alive. The absolute reality is life — the rest is form and appearance; and I am reconciled to death because I feel and am persuaded that it is but the dark and awful gateway to wider worlds and larger life.

They who have best known how to express the vital and essential truths are the great teachers and the great masters of style.

My private benefit is no benefit at all. If it is to be a joy and a blessing to me, it must be shared; and though my work bring me but disappointment and care, yet if I feel that for others it shall become the source of inner freedom and strength, for myself also it is converted into wealth and power.

If thou exalt thyself thou compellest remembrance of the hideousness of thy baser nature;

but if thou art reverent, mild, and helpful, the wise and the good will think only of thy heavenly descent and destiny.

As in a herd, when a few wallow in the mire all are made filthy by contact, so are the innocent defiled by evil company.

Loyalty is to principles, and to persons only in so far as they are symbols and representatives of principles.

Objections to what increases in the multitude the power of reason and conscience are not worth considering unless we are prepared to think that conscious life is a curse. Nor are the objections to the inventions and contrivances which enable ever-growing multitudes to gain a livelihood with less labor and toil of any weight. The large and deep view shows us that democratic government, popular education, machinery and capital, all co-operate with religion to lift mankind to higher and broader levels, though the evils incident to the process may at times appear to overbalance the good.

The harmony which is produced by fear or greed will break into discord so soon as the danger or occasion has passed. A permanent union can be based only on permanent principle and interests. Hence the only secure foundation of national peace and prosperity is religion, morality, and justice; and the greater the freedom and intelligence the greater the need of these conservative forces.

Egotism and heroism exclude each other. The hero thinks not of himself, but he gives all he has, his very life, for what he loves more than himself. The egotist is bound up within himself. He loves his safety, his ease, his comfort, his pleasure, and he clings to them, though to do so he have to sacrifice truth, justice, and honor, good name and friends, and whatever else a noble soul holds to be most precious. He has neither patriotism nor religion, neither a great mind nor a generous heart, but tethered like a beast he moves in a narrow circle whose centre is his shrivelled self; and in seeking what may minister to his idolatry he loses both the sense of the worth of life and the power to enjoy its sweetest blessings.

Life is said to be dull and monotonous, and yet its variety is so endless that it is never the same for any two human beings; and for each one it varies from day to day and from year to year. The sameness lies in our heavy sluggish natures, and if we arouse and make ourselves alive we find infinite entertainment.

## II.

THE power of habit may be seen in those whom it reconciles to things nature shrinks from — in undertakers, grave-diggers, butchers, scavengers, and all who work in filth and ordure. It is habit that creates for each one a separate world which he finds pleasant or endurable. It enables those who dwell in the midst of deserts and rocks and everlasting snows to adapt themselves to their surroundings and love their homes. It is habit that endears the ocean to the sailor, the forest to the savage, the cell to the hermit, the sanctuary to the worshipper, and the book to the student. Whatever kind of life commends itself to man as good and desirable, habit will enable him to lead. If it be a life to which money is indispensable, the habit of industry and economy will procure him riches; if it be a life of knowledge and virtue the habit of study and right-doing will secure them for him. Its force extends to the whole circle of human affairs.

It regulates the course of our daily actions, determines when we shall sleep and when we shall wake, when we shall sit at table and when we shall rise. It decides what work we shall do, what games we shall play. A complete theory of habituation would be the sum of practical wisdom, a comprehensive system of pedagogics, and a safe guide for whoever occupies himself with education. If a man is perfectible it is because he is habituable. If he is corrupt or perverse it is because good habits have not been formed in him by those who influenced and controlled his childhood and youth; for whoever can be led astray is capable under right guidance of accustoming himself to a life of honor and virtue.

The saying, Be great and be miserable, may be true of those whom wealth or position distinguishes, but not of those whom mind and character raise and confirm.

The meditator even in the midst of the most pleasant company is like an exile who though surrounded by the noblest monuments and the fairest scenes of foreign lands still dreams of home.

They who live for pleasure live without joy.

So long as the fountain within flows strong and clear we believe and know and feel that life is good; for from this inner source when it runs pure and full, faith and hope, love and joy rise as freely as fragrance from the flowers when they bloom.

We are capable of taking interest in others to the extent in which we feel ourselves to be interesting.

Of all habits that which it is most needful to acquire is the habit of striving consciously and ceaselessly to improve, to surpass one's self, to grow in wisdom and grace, to develop within one's self higher and higher quality and potency of life.

A habit of carefulness in all things is one of the best results of right education.

If we are asked why the drunkard, the lecher, the liar, and the thief do not reform we reply that it is because they are the victims of habit; and the same answer is to be given if the question be why the rich are still eager to add to their wealth.

A man may live content in darkness and captivity if within there shine the light which gladdens the soul.

One cannot know whether his work shall have been done in vain. Whatever happen, he must continue to strive or he will sink into hebetude and nullity. Let each one therefore do with all his might as though God had poised the world's welfare on his single will.

Not what is, still less what is known, but what imagination bodies forth makes the world in which each one of us lives, to which nothing but faith, desire, and love give meaning and worth. In losing our illusions, unless some nobler dream take their place, we lose relish for life.

No power can save fools and sinners from the consequences of their sin and folly; and were this not so, there would perhaps be none but fools and sinners.

Evil is everything which weakens admiration, reverence, and love.

Still seek to learn, but let thy first and final aim be to get wisdom and virtue, for if they be lacking, knowledge is vanity.

From slime to slime along slimy ways, and for the rest mere nothingness in the bosom of the eternally unconscious. This is the atheist's sum of all we are and know. But however men may live, such a creed must forever be incredible.

The complete attainment of truth, goodness, and beauty is the end of life; faith, hope, and love the means.

The more unselfish and unenvious we are the

larger the world in which we are able to live with sympathy and delight.

Thy virtues are all the more real the less thou thinkest of them; but thy vices thou canst not study too assiduously.

The love-winning force of one's religion and piety is no uncertain test of their truth and genuineness.

Make thyself wise and good, and thou shalt know that there is no joy but in being useful.

Religion is a food or a medicine. If those who partake of the food are made healthful and vigorous; if those who take the medicine are cured of their ills, we are persuaded that they are wholesome and efficacious; and so when those who accept the doctrines and follow the practices prescribed by religion are wise, chaste, mild, generous, cheerful, brave, and large-minded, their manner of life commends their faith better than arguments. There is, however, a perversity of human nature which shuts out the view of goodness when it is a virtue of those whom we dislike.

The important thing is not what we know, but what knowledge is a vital element in our thinking and doing.

The good do right because righteousness is God's will, the command of reason, the law of conscience, the purpose, aim, and end of life, since it is life. To do good in the hope of pleasing others is by implication a denial of the supreme worth of truth and virtue.

Life is cut in two by the line of sex, and by the union of the sexes it is reconstituted and propagated. In the case of man the Christian religion and the consent of the wise teach that except in wedlock this union is defilement and desecration. But even in wedlock it is a perversion and degradation whenever the one purpose by which it is sanctified is absent. The incontinence of the married weakens and lowers the race more than prostitution and adultery; for these are condemned and opposed by all the good, while the cowardly and ignoble indulgences of the wedded are covered by the mantle of respectability and the fiction which sanctions whatever is customary or legal, though it be robbery and murder.

The weakness which attacks our weakness is more to be dreaded than the strength which challenges us our strength.

Since thou canst become able to do whatever thou canst accustom thyself to do, occupy thyself habitually with the best things.

All things are brought into relief by contrast — truth by error, religion by impiety, intelligence by ignorance; and where this opposition is not found the tendency is to lower and lower levels. What but depravity can arouse and sustain enthusiasm for good? How should the heart be stirred to sympathy and beneficence if there were no poverty and wretchedness? What but unbelief and indifference can awaken and keep alive zeal for the conversion and reformation of men? Be not discouraged then by the evil which is everywhere around thee, but know that it exists to urge thee to a more human, a more godlike life.

For whole days no illumining thought smiles on me, like a star from the bosom of darkness, and when I turn to the words of the great masters they seem to be flat and unprofitable. This is doubtless the settled state of all who are indifferent to the things of the spirit. They have ears and hear not; eyes and see not. To such as they the Saviour spoke, foreseeing that the heavenly seed would not take root and bear fruit. No divine persuasiveness, no miraculous power can startle them from out the lethargy in which matter has steeped their souls.

One's own experience is the sole means whereby he can determine for himself whether a thing be true or useful or delectable or beautiful. This applies to mathematical truth as to the deliciousness of fruit and the fragrance of flowers. Without experience there is no knowledge, since the primal element in thought is feeling, which is experience. If one know what he has not felt, accepting it on trust, his knowledge is real only in so far as his faith is grounded on experience. They who have not suffered are ignorant, because the deepest wisdom is brought home to us through experience, not of what is pleasant, but of what hurts and drives us back on ourselves and God. No one is great in mind or character who has not greatly endured, because endurance is the chosen school of experience. They who are unwilling or unable to bear are unwilling or unable to learn. They who have a rich experience of small things, investigating, weighing, comparing, and doing them, with all care and seriousness, are made wise and strong, because life is made up of minutes and minutiæ, which seem not worth considering, but which if rightly taken issue in incredible power and repose.

Consistency is a virtue of the unprogressive.

Contentment with one's self is harmful; but to be content with what one possesses is often the surest sign of wisdom.

"Why," asks Scipio, "shouldst thou desire to be known to posterity, since thou art unknown to those who died before thy birth, who are neither less numerous nor less worthy?" But may not one believe that the noble dead still have consciousness of the spirits akin to their own who yet strive on earth? Or if not so, is there not all the stronger motive to make one's self a man and do deeds which shall be remembered by those who follow?

As an individual turns from his defects and exaggerates his qualities, so does an age. In the most barbarous the belief has prevailed that they were enlightened; and a few hundred years hence, historians may prove that the nineteenth century was an epoch of decadence in which man's higher powers, his imagination, his conscience, his will, even his intellect declined from the vigor of happier times.

Strong minds cannot long continue in meditation, and the many are incapable of serious thought. Hence spiritual truth which moulds our life only when it is wrought into our being by our own self-activity has but slight hold on the masses, who are swayed and dominated by interests and passions which concern their present existence alone. If they are to be brought under the influence of ideal aims and ends, these ideals must be associated with their practical affairs. If they are to be religious, they must be made to feel that in religion they shall find comfort and strength, peace and joy, hope and courage — effectual help in doing the things which now occupy them. Their religion must ally itself therefore with their love of home, of country, of property, of security, of health of mind and body.

As we believe those who tell us what they have seen in their travels, so we believe in a more living way those who tell us what patient study and meditation have revealed to them. Thus a few lead the whole world to accept as masterpieces the great works of art, poetry, philosophy, and science.

One should be willing to see his foes and rivals surpass him, if only he be enabled thereby to rise above all envious thoughts.

No one can teach or govern or influence man or beast in a wholesome way unless he take interest in his work and love the good his labors produce.

If thou art prevented from doing the thing thou hast proposed, do some better thing.

If the best is thine — faith in God and in the worth of life, wisdom and knowledge, courage and patience, goodness and love of truth, — it is impossible thou shouldst envy another his possessions.

Greed and sensuality undermine self-respect, because each one feels that the spirit of man is superior to matter and becomes ignoble when it suffers itself to be cowed and enslaved by what is external.

The dissolute and abandoned, who are accustomed to insult and outrage, become insensible to such treatment, but may be touched and helped when approached in the spirit of sympathy and loving-kindness.

Should one who fills us with admiration and reverence reveal himself as a liar, a lecher, or a thief, the blow would be felt as more painful than if a friend whose approach we had greeted with unfeigned joy should, as we stretch a hand to welcome him, make a brutal assault upon us.

When we dissect the body, laying bare its whole muscular, nervous, and bony tissue, and exposing to view all the vital organs, it becomes a thing hideous, loathsome, and dead. Now this is what our processes of analysis do for knowledge and faith; and when all has been taken apart or dissolved into abstractions, the mind, like the dissected body, becomes a chaos, where nothing seems supreme but confusion.

To make perpetual vows under the influence of passionate love is as irrational as to assume lasting obligations in a state of drunkenness.

If our pity, our sympathy, were doubly as strong, they would make life unbearable.

To give money is an act of doubtful morality, for giving tends rather to harm than to improve the receiver. The most it were wise to do is to care for those whom not even necessity can drive to self-help.

We know of the world and even of our most intimate friends only the impressions they make upon us.

The mystery in which each separate thing is involved is the same that veils the universe of which it is part. We comprehend neither subject nor object.

Live not to enjoy, but to improve thyself, and it shall be well with thee.

Give to me, O God, the good which is Thyself, which the more it is communicated, the more all-sufficient it is felt to be; and teach me not to set my heart on aught which can be mine only at another's cost.

Freedom is better than success; yet hardly shall we find one who is not ready to barter liberty for place.

Once we realize that the human race, in its visible manifestation at least, is ephemeral, as evanescent as the extinct species of past geologic epochs, we are fatally driven by the spirit which is a man's self into unseen worlds where what is true and good and fair abides forever, though the panoramic universe vanish utterly.

Since it is possible to find happiness in loving wife and children and friends, whether or not we believe them to be immortal, why may we not attain the good of life in loving the human race, though we are certain it shall wholly disappear? Reply without fear that the happiness born of the love of what is transitory is but a sort of comfortableness, which is for the moment and without power to still the thoughts and yearnings that wander through eternity and are the utterance of man's true and inmost being.

The love of children for parents, of brothers and sisters for one another, is due to habits of intimacy and helpfulness, and not to ties of blood. This is seen in the case of those who, adopted in infancy, have been brought up in the belief that their foster parents were their fathers and mothers, or that they were brothers and sisters, when, in fact, they were not akin. The love then, which above all other we persuade ourselves springs from natural affinity, is but a thing of custom.

Even the fearless may be overcome by terror, as they may be struck helpless by sword or shell.

The things and persons that provoke and annoy us are but occasions. The cause lies in our weakness and selfishness.

The happiness of the young is made possible by their ignorance of the miseries of life, of the indifference, cruelty, and injustice of the world — an ignorance which instruction is powerless to destroy, which in the noblest, experience itself fails to dispel.

Thou art able to do good to whomever thou livest with in daily intercourse. Whether to others thou canst hardly know.

Let the attitude of others toward thee have little influence on thy conduct. Thy desire is to act in obedience to eternal laws, to do permanent good, and why shouldst thou be turned aside by the ignorance or the prejudice of those who would hinder thee? If thou art a real man, the lowlier the place the greater the opportunity.

The most generous deed arouses little enthusiasm, when it is, by implication even, an appeal to ourselves to be generous.

How easily even the good become criminal when they are persuaded that nothing but crime can procure what they intensely desire or save them from what they greatly dread!

Whoever can influence men should strive

to make them courageous, enduring, hopeful, simple, self-active, chaste.

The man and the woman attract each other, but unless they are drawn and held by some higher and more stable force than sexual passion, they soon find that to be bound in wedlock is to be enslaved.

Woman's deepest and tenderest love is wholly removed from sensual thoughts. It is the love mothers give to their children, daughters to fathers, the best and the noblest to the men they admire, trust, and adore.

Whatever helps us to turn from ease and pleasure, and to submit to labor and self-denial, whether it be the love of money, or of reputation, or of culture, or of virtue, is wholesome and good. The love of excellence and power is human; enslavement to appetite and instinct is brutish.

The sage and the saint pass unnoticed; the rich and the high-placed awaken envious thoughts.

As a small room may be more full of comfort and joy than a palace, so he who in obscurity lives for truth and love is more blessed than one who lacking inner freedom and light is applauded by thousands.

God's will is the welfare and salvation of

mankind. Human interests, therefore, are supreme.

The points of view to which we accustom ourselves shape and color so largely the objects which make the world of consciousness possible, that it is inevitable men should hold, as times and circumstances change, various and even opposite beliefs, opinions, and convictions concerning religion, philosophy, government, and whatever else is related to their lives. But as there are right and wrong points of view, so there are true and false opinions, beliefs, and convictions.

A self is one who exists and is an object for himself, who therefore is at once subject and object. The self as object is the self as subject, reinforced and transformed by all that one knows, desires, loves, or hates — by the totality of the experience which is made possible by the external world, but which as experience is part of the inner life. It is this that makes self-education feasible.

The uniformity of nature is uniformity of experience.

One would not wish to be an inanimate object, however fair; for if what has no life is of worth, it is so only for the living. One would not wish to be a flower, however beautiful or fragrant;

for it can be beautiful or fragrant only for those who have senses. One would not wish to be a mere animal, however noble or strong, for whatever its courage or strength it cannot be conscious of the possession of its qualities. It is consciousness, then, that gives value, and in a world in which there should be no conscious being, there could be no truth, no goodness, no beauty.

Since to be a man is to think and love, they who think and love the highest things are the best. The objection may be opposed that to be a man one must eat and drink, and that they who eat and drink the best things are the best. Yes, if the ideal be eating and drinking, and the perfect good be found in the indulgence of appetite. But to hold this is to believe animality better than humanity, digestion than emotion, desire than love, instinct than reason.

It is God's world. He takes care of it, and He has made me that I too may have share in the divine work, even as the slightest atom has its place in the harmony of the universe.

The vast voraciousness of mankind is appalling to one whose faith is spiritual. The plains and the seas, the forests and the heavens do not suffice to satisfy appetites, which the more they are indulged the more clamorous they become.

Men when hungry are as ravenous as beasts of prey. They rob, they murder, they burn cities, they lay waste whole regions; and when they are satiated they set about getting more savory dishes, more delicious wines. If their stomachs urge them on, poverty, shame, and disease have no terrors for them. Feed them and give them copious drink and they are your slaves. Ask them to abstain, and though you promise the divinest joys that may be born of high thoughts and exalted emotions, they will hate and revile you.

To think and love is life; to see, to hear, to taste, to digest, to excrete, is but existence. They who think are the only noblemen and lords. They are the masters of all they know, have overcome whatever they understand. They dwell apart in a kingdom of their own, where they lead the life of immortals, occupying themselves with the things that are eternal, loving the beauty which is fadeless and everduring.

Sight and hearing are nobler senses than touch, more intimately related to intellectual and social life, but they fail to create the conviction of reality which is born of contact and palpation. They make us victims of hallucination. Visionary means fanciful, dreamlike, unsubstantial; and delusion lurks in sound, which distracts, takes captive, and leads astray. But what we grasp and firmly hold we cannot doubt to be real more than we can doubt the reality of our existence. If, however, by analysis or other process, we strive to get at the essence of things, what we touch, no less than what we see and hear, dissolves and vanishes, becoming, if considered subjectively, but sensation; if objectively, but appearance.

Experience cannot transcend itself, and if it seem to do so, a deeper view shows such transcendence to be in reality immanence. If we find not God within ourselves we shall find Him nowhere.

The adage, What we do not know we cannot crave, is true; but it is also true that the objects of experience are primarily objects of desire or aversion rather than objects of knowledge. They are first presented to us as things interesting and serviceable or indifferent and harmful; and the fact that they must therefore be intelligible is implied, not affirmed, in consciousness. Hence, if teaching is not to be without effect, a longing for the things which education promises to give must be awakened in the pupil. More than knowledge must be held out to him; and vulgar success cannot be proposed, unless we wish to blight what is finest and fairest in him. The love of knowledge for its own sake can be but the final result of the best culture, and to lure the young with the hope of money or office is to lead them astray. The end of life is not thought, but thought fulfilling itself in right deeds. Hence the teacher, if he is an educator, must bring his pupils to realize that the faculties which nothing but education can produce are indispensable to the best life without which the highest joy and blessedness is impossible.

Education is not a product: it is a process; and the universal failure of schools is attributable chiefly to the persuasion of teachers that their business is to turn out products, and not to start, stimulate, and direct processes of self-activity which shall continue as long as life.

How easily the poet, the philosopher, and the saint pass beyond the confines of the world of things palpable and scientifically demonstrable, into the presence of the eternal and absolute, where, as in their proper home, they dream, love, and adore.

Neither knowledge nor nescience is absolute. They are correlative and interfused. We do not know the whole of anything; and since whatever is, is intelligible, there is nothing of which we do not know something, if only this, that to be at all, it must be in harmony with the laws of mind. What cannot be known cannot and does not exist. All faith, hope, and love rest, however vaguely, on a basis of knowledge. Were it possible to be conscious at all of what can in no way be known, the attitude of reason toward such a being would be that of infinite indifference and aloofness.

He who exacts even love for love does not love; for true love gives all and asks nothing in return but the privilege and blessedness of loving. If I know and love the best, it matters little whether the best know and love me; but if I know and love God, it is because He knows and loves me.

The power to interest permanently lies not in things, but in persons—in their faith and knowledge, their hopes and fears, their efforts, successes, and failures, their courage and love. This is what the highest art bodies forth; this is what the poet sings, the orator proclaims, the painter portrays, the historian recounts, the story-writer tells. This is the theme of conversation whenever the divine awakens within us and the soul has free utterance. Facts and laws are as monotonous as sleep, as heavy as eating and drinking. We are spirits, and what delights us is the spirit's play.

To know is higher than to feel; to do right is higher than to know; and to compel feeling, knowledge, and conduct into the service of the soul, as through faith, hope, and love, it struggles Godward, is the highest within man's reach.

I seek a principle which shall reconcile me to all things; a principle which shall enable me to accept evil as I accept good, and to be content whatever befall. I can find but this: whatever happens, through whatever agencies, happens by the will or the permission of God, who creates me, knows me, has care of me; and who, since He is all-wise and all-loving, will not permit me to suffer loss or harm unless it be that I may find richer gain or higher good.

God is with each one, whether or not he seek and know Him, trust and love Him. As man's thought does not create Him, it is powerless to restrain or abolish His action in the world. They who deny His being confess that being when they utter truth, believe in right, and follow after goodness. If they rise to heaven, He is there; if they sink to the depths of hell, He is there. He is greater than our knowledge of Him: greater than our faith or hope or love can intimate, and to think to limit His power and goodness is to blaspheme. What we know best is our own ignorance and unworthiness; and here too our thoughts are not God's thoughts.

Since what I am I have become why shall I not hope still to grow Godward?

Be persuaded that whatever truth or virtue is any man's may be thine.

Had I the fame of Plato or Shakespeare I should deem it no benefit unless I could account it the approval of God.

Wisdom is not born of learning, but may be found in simple minds; while they who know many things often lack judgment and sanity.

Nature is God's manifest and universal fact; to contemn it is blasphemy not less than folly.

Courage, strength, virility win not admiration merely, but love — the love not of women only but of men as well.

True lovers of peace find it easy to live in peace with their fellow-men. By their very bearing and temper they disarm foes, silence the envious, and shame the contentious and turbulent into acquiescence.

So long as one is able to inspire hope and courage, so long is it a joy for him to be alive.

The saddest is not the loss of hope, but the loss of the power to desire aught — to feel that there is nothing any human being might say or do, which could stir within us even a momentary thrill of pleasure.

It may be thought that if our belief in the immortality of the soul were real, we should not grieve when death takes those we love. But we sorrow when they leave us to dwell in other lands, though we are certain that there also they shall be alive. The father suffers when his daughter quits his home to follow the man she has wedded, though he knows that she has found happiness. To part from those who are dear is pain even when we feel the separation is for their good. We pity our friends who die less than ourselves for being deprived of the cheer and comfort they gave. Death is sad because life is sweet; and it would still be sad could we have positive proof that the dead relive in better worlds.

Unless one be a child or a savage, a youth or a barbarian, it is not possible to take pleasure in what gives pain to any living thing.

Avarice is a passion of those who, doubting the reality of the spiritual world, incapable of love or devotion, and distrusting their own souls, clutch matter and hold to it unto death with the grip of despair.

In childhood and youth we look to a father or a mother to reassure and comfort us in our doubts and sorrows, feeling certain that they have the will, the knowledge, and the ability to guide and protect us. As we advance in years we still turn to some one in whom we believe there is superior strength, wisdom, and goodness. The disciple follows the master, the soldier, his captain. Most of our beliefs and opinions rest on the authority of those whom we hold to be wise and good; and when we have attained best insight we put our whole trust in God, in His love and mercy and tender care, throwing all our weight of sin and woe on Him who makes and saves us, and will not suffer us to perish utterly.

Weeping and lamentation are of no avail; and are therefore meaningless and idle. The worst misfortunes are endurable, if we but have strength of mind and put our trust in God.

As there are animals which habit makes able to see in the dark, so long and patient meditation gives the power to see clear where others are blind.

If one could have the boundless devotion which the purest and most loving souls have given to the Saviour, but should himself be false and base, the worship of the world would leave him miserable.

The pretentious are necessarily ridiculous.

The larger the world we consciously live in, the greater our freedom and tranquillity.

One is not better for belonging to a powerful family or nation; but he has greater opportunities.

One may become indifferent to praise, but hardly to the voice of the faultfinder.

The good are content when they do good and are not troubled because the credit is given to others.

What we have grown accustomed to does not appear to us to be ridiculous or absurd, though it often is so.

The race exists for the individual: the individual for the race only in so far as it is the indispensable means of producing personalities — the final end of the universe which is the work of a supreme Person.

The creative minds who live in literature are neither young nor old. They are forever in their prime, safe harbored from the follies of youth, the decrepitude of age, and all the accidents of disaster-working time. They stand on the threshold of the centuries, to welcome the noblest and the best, as, from generation to generation, they step forth to play their parts on life's stage.

At times the weight of years seems to drop from me and again I stand with a boy's eager and all-hoping heart beneath the azure sky of May, while the companions of my youth spring from the earth like flowers to fill the world with light and joy. But when awakening as from a dream I see that the leaves have fallen, that the birds have flown, that the friends of other days have departed, my heart turns to God, to the eternal fountain of everduring life and love.

Can there be worse folly than to sacrifice freedom, peace of mind, opportunity to live within and to grow godlike, that one may get a title or live in splendor and luxury? Not for this, it may be said, but for greater power to be of help. Never yet, alas! has this been the true motive of vain and ambitious men, who, whether they have acted in the name of religion or of patriotism, have still sought themselves.

The questions which concern a man as a member of whatever social organism are superficial and uninteresting, in comparison with those which touch the root of his being and relate him to God and eternal things.

So to live, so to utter one's life in words and deeds, as to be borne from generation to generation, in the grateful memories, in the admiring and loving thoughts of the wisest and best, is to have an unending triumph, is the only right apotheosis.

The young walk in the midst of the many-tinted, rich-glowing clouds of Illusion, which, as experience and insight increase, lose their bright colors and at last turn ashen gray. But the noblest souls, though they see the beauty and the glory fade, lose nor heart nor hope, but gird themselves for more heroic strivings to attain the divine reality, of which they feel these early visions were but shadows.

It saddens to think of the poverty, discomforts, and hardships of millions of human beings; but their real misery lies in their ignorance, sensuality, cowardice, and selfishness, in their indifference to the things of the soul, in their lack of love.

Untoward happenings are changed to good fortune when they teach courage, forbearance, and wisdom.

One who is wholly in earnest in the persevering pursuit of any worthy object can never be commonplace.

Unless I may learn of thee or teach thee wisdom and virtue, I care not for thy company.

Though divinity and immortality were, like the words themselves, but abstractions, it would still be the highest wisdom to live for God and life everlasting.

Whatever hinders or distracts from the divine work of purifying the soul and laboring with all one's strength to be of help, is calamity. Throw the whole stress of thy life on the inner self.

"And to you, Verus, what seems the noblest end of life?" Quietly and gravely he replied, "The imitation of God."

The chief end of study is the learning to think, and the best books therefore are those which most effectually impel to exercise of mind.

As the sense of the worth and sacredness of life diminishes, men abandon themselves to selfish impulses, to the pursuit of wealth or pleasure, looking on all else as illusory. They become hard or sensual, incapable of conceiving or of cherishing noble purposes or ideal aims. Hence an age in which the sense of the worth and sacredness of life is failing is decadent, however great the material prosperity and progress.

In true workers method and order are economies of time. But they also help the idle to persuade themselves that the void and vacancy of their lives are filled; for those who are busy doing useless things easily imagine, if they have method and order, that they are occupied with what is worth while.

Great souls cannot content themselves with trifles, but turn from what is ephemeral or nugatory to the unseen world, where all is enduring and real. They look away from the present in which children and the unthinking live, to the future, and strive to have thoughts and do deeds worthy of immortal beings.

## III.

THE love of repose, of order, of a uniform and even course of life would seem to spring from a rational and virtuous disposition, but it is often a result of sloth and selfishness, or of timidity and cowardice; and it may therefore be found in those who seek their ease and comfort at whatever cost, who if they are too indifferent to hate, are too indolent to help. They will not trouble themselves to right wrongs or prevent ills, but suffer things to take their way. They little care what happens if only they be not disturbed. They are incapable of generous emotions and are without noble impulses. If they are clothed with authority they correct no abuses, oppose no obstacles to the downward tendency of the many when left to themselves. They ignore the corruption which gives them no annoyance; and if it be urged on their attention, they consider those who denounce it as officious or impertinent. They would be thought wise and able for doing nothing, and they hold in slight esteem the active, energetic, and zealous, whose example is a rebuke to their own lethargy and inertness. This self-indulgent weakness and love of ease in the men who govern, whether in Church or State, has wrought greater ruin than the scoffings of infidels and the scandals of the vicious: for all understand that unbelievers will mock and that scandals must be; but that they who are placed as guardians over treasures of infinite price should fall asleep and slumber on while thieves break in and steal seems a thing monstrous and incredible to those who have faith in God and the soul. When the weak and careless are appointed to do what only the strong and vigilant can perform, confusion or ruin is inevitable.

When work has become a habit one is lost without it, as the drunkard without his dram, the gambler without his game.

The divinest things — religion, love, truth, beauty, justice — seem to lose their meaning and value when we sink into lassitude and indifference. In such mental state we, together with what is not ourselves, verge in consciousness toward the confines where all that is or has been or can be appears shadowy and unsubstantial. It is a state altogether different from that of the callous and dull, who have no perception of spiritual truth, no definite notions of anything. It is in fact not a state, but a passing obscuration, a moral syncope, a temporary inability to think or love or hope or take delight in aught. It is a signal that we should quit meditation and books, and go out into the open air, into the presence of nature, into the company of flocks and children, where we may drink new health and vigor from the clear and full-flowing fountains of life, afar from the arid wastes of theory and speculation; where we may learn again that it is not by intellectual questionings, but by believing, hoping, loving, and doing that man finds joy and peace.

What a man is he has become. He is born wholly helpless, incapable of surviving for even a brief space without the aid and assistance of beings in whom intelligence has been developed; and what we consider his natural endowments are for the most part products of art. Nothing, for instance, plays a greater rôle in life and literature than the love of man for woman — the mysterious and all-absorbing passion which bribes or overpowers reason, which thrusts aside the usual motives that influence conduct, which compels those whom it subdues to forget religion, country, parents, and friends; driving heroes to forego honor and glory, sages to forsake wisdom, saints to abandon God. This strange fascination, this marvellous attraction, is not, as one might suppose, a thing of sex and the senses: it is romantic, imaginative, poetic; it is all compact of revery and fancy; it is a product of art, not of nature; a result of civilization, not of instinct. It could not exist among savages who go naked. With them it is simply sexual desire little different from that found in brutes. It arises only when the body is clothed and adorned, habited in mystery, and converted into a thing hidden and sacred, which appeals to the imagination and leads it to build, for the divinity which itself has created, a sanctuary wherein it may worship until the winning of the favor of the goddess becomes the supreme end of life, wherein to fail is to be doomed to misery. So the beloved becomes at once an ideal and an idol. But the divine frenzy is born of vesture, of manner, of artifice, of concealment, and of mystery. Take these away and the madness is cured.

> Loosed the girdle and the veil,
> All the heavenly dream grows pale.

They who are drawn together by sexual passion or by interest are not attracted by love, but by instinct or selfishness, and when desire has been satiated or the advantage sought has been gained, they separate, not without loathing or contempt; for it is natural to despise or hate those whom we have made use of whether for gain or lust.

The most blissful moments are those we pass in adoration, or in writing the thoughts that blossom from the roots of our being, which dip into infinite and everduring worlds.

From nature we receive little more than dispositions. For the rest, what we become is the result of circumstances and the co-operation of the will, which is generally determined by environment and chance happenings. All depends on God's providence and grace, but the ways along which He guides us are mysterious and hidden, even after we have passed over them. A mere nothing, whose import we could not have understood, would have changed the whole course of life for any one of us. Things light as straws shape our purposes. If experience teaches anything, it is that we should keep ourselves free of conceit and be slow to judge our fellows.

How many submit to the restraints of society and comply with its requirements for no other reason than because such a course is safer, more respectable, and more certain to lead to success!

Much of our virtue, indeed, is as little part of ourselves as are our clothes, and is as easily divested when the social atmosphere or the moral climate changes.

However eager men be for the contest, victors and vanquished alike quickly grow indifferent once it is over. In the triumph there is less joy, in the defeat less disappointment than either could have believed possible. It is so in trials of strength and skill; it is so in the great struggles on which the fates of armies and of nations hang. The keenest delight is anticipatory. When the issue is decided, when what had been a possibility becomes a fact, our interest relaxes, and we turn to the undetermined, which gives free play to the imagination and an open field to hope. So too we find that the death of our dearest friends, the vanishing of our most cherished illusions, without which life had seemed to be meaningless, are not unbearable. However great the loss, in a boundless universe there is always something left to believe, to strive for, and to love.

Whatever may be true of the uneducated, they whose pursuits are intellectual should need no other diversion or relaxation than they may find in their studies; and they whose vocation obliges them to deal with religious truth can consent to pass their time at games and other entertainments only when they have lost faith in the reality of the spiritual world.

Strength, physical, intellectual, and moral, is desirable, if for no other reason, because only the strong can be generous, helpful, and magnanimous. The weak shrink into themselves, nurse their sorrows, emphasize their sufferings and wrongs, and so become complaining, selfish, and exacting. They are the centre of their thoughts and indifferent to the interests of others. They understand no ills but their own. If they listen to pitiful stories it is that they get a keener relish for their proper miseries, with which they seem to be in love. They are without gratitude and are incapable of appreciating kindnesses. The strong, on the contrary, if they are not brutal, find happiness in sharing their strength and joy. Their sympathies are deep, and they are eager to make others partakers of the blessings bestowed so largely on themselves.

Self-love, in the true sense, is the love of one's real good — of truth, of virtue, of beauty, of God. It is strongest in those who are most alive in their higher nature. It is the opposite of selfish love, of the love which places the chief good in the things which minister to the senses or nourish conceit and pride, and not in what constitutes the proper worth and joy of life.

Why should I desire that others think as I, that they take interest in what interests me? If all were of one mind, if all had the same tastes, life would be less interesting than it is; and then it is plain that they who have not my experience cannot have my thoughts, that they who have not my character cannot have my tastes. Nevertheless I would bring others to accept the truth I know, to admire and follow the beauty and goodness which I see; and this yearning springs from what is best within me, from God's presence in my soul, impelling me to reveal to my brothers Him who is truth, beauty, and goodness.

The power which habit has over us is shown in the fact that the things we become accustomed to in our earliest years, — the scenes, the songs, the beliefs, the prejudices even, — however much we may recognize that the value we attributed to them was due chiefly to our own ignorance and crudeness, never cease to be dear.

Having done all thou canst do, await the event with a calm mind. Whatever it be, thou art blameless, and safe therefore from harm.

If we except the present instant, which is

gone before we can call attention to it, all time is past, since the future does not exist. What is past has ceased to be; and the whole of life, therefore, is summed in an instant, which — if we try to think of it — vanishes. It is this that gives insight into the illusiveness, the evanescence, the emptiness, the futility of temporal existence, driving the soul back on itself and impelling it to seek escape from annihilation in the bosom of the Eternal, in whom, and not in time, it truly lives. Hence the old, though they clearly see that they have but a little while to remain on earth, still continue to plan, to provide, to prolong hope, and to cherish expectation. Though they know it not, they are already dwellers in eternity.

Only the greatest minds greatly influence us, and not even they unless with much toil and patience we work our way into the heart of their thought and love.

The good are cautious and irresolute, and therefore the affairs of the world are delivered over to the bold and unscrupulous, who have neither the will nor the ability to accomplish anything of enduring worth.

The child lives wholly in the present and is influenced solely by what is to happen now. The youth begins to look to the future but does not labor with joy for rewards which are distant. It is a mark of maturity when we grow able to live by hope, to toil on through whatever difficulties and obstacles, strengthened by the thought and expectation of what we shall be or have when years will have passed by. But the wisest and the strongest alone understand that right action is its own sufficient blessing, that to do day by day the best one can do is the highest and sweetest life, whatever may come hereafter.

The welfare and happiness of those around us as servants and neighbors give us small concern, and yet we persuade ourselves that we love our country and all mankind; are foolish enough even to imagine that we are capable of making sacrifices to promote the good of those who shall be born a hundred years hence.

The rich and the office-holders receive greater benefits from society and the institutions by which it is maintained than the multitude; and hence they are voluble in professions of patriotism and of respect for law, though in truth they generally love their country less and are more willing to evade the duties of citizenship than the masses of the people, being corrupted by money and by office.

The wholly sincere are bewildered and lost

in the midst of a world of pretence, and would flee from the monstrous all-pervading lie to solitude and the presence of God.

The most perfect beauty, that which bears the divinest charm and is clothed with the sweetest grace, eludes our utmost endeavor to understand its nature. We feel its presence, are subdued by its power, worship at its shrine, but whether it be found in the human countenance or in a poem or a painting, in a statue or a musical composition, we know not what it is; and could the veil of mystery be lifted the spell would be broken.

Men are followed and flattered for their money, their position, their power to confer honor or office, for their titles and social distinctions; and when they are sought for themselves, it is not for their natural, but for their acquired qualities, — for their skill in law or medicine, in oratory or music, for their fine manners, their knowledge of polite usages, or their ability to entertain. What is inborn, — as a healthful and vigorous constitution or physical beauty, — however much it may be cherished by its possessors, has of itself small social value. A man is not esteemed or rewarded for his strength, but for the uses he has taught himself to put it to; not for what nature has given him, but for what art has made him. Physical beauty may attract individuals of opposite sex, but it is held to be a danger or a doubtful good unless it be associated with intelligence, refinement, and moral worth. One's value, then, as a social being depends not on what he has received from nature, but on what education has made of him.

That man should be able to know and realize his own insignificance; that he, a being of a day, an atom swallowed in immensity, should be capable of thoughts which wander through eternity, of hopes and loves which touch on infinity, is the most indisputable evidence of his heavenly descent and nature; and we are prepared to find that the profoundest minds have best insight into the essential littleness of human life, the deepest sentiment of its utter vanity, when it is considered merely as a fact of time.

They who lead the life of meditation and aspiration find such peace and joy therein that they little by little lose the power to take interest in the ambitions, struggles, and intrigues which are the substance of history. It all becomes for them but as the meaningless agitations of the mobile and noisy crowd.

The ancient philosophers theorized, speculated, and argued: the modern observe, experiment, and induce conclusions. This method they apply to everything from matter to sensation and thought; but the farther they advance the wider and deeper the realms of nescience open before them. So their larger knowledge clamors for a larger faith.

They who make us laugh make themselves ridiculous; and therefore we have a secret contempt for jesters, mimics, comedians, and clowns. It is difficult to take seriously those who amuse us. In the courts of feudal lords and kings the providers of merriment were accounted fools. However willing we may be to pay for such entertainment, we do not respect the individuals by whom it is furnished. Laughter is at the expense of others, and is generally provoked by what makes them appear awkward, absurd, or inferior. A smile may be full of approval, encouragement, and love; but laughter is more apt to be unfeeling, mocking, and bitter; or if not so, it bespeaks a vacant mind, and is loudest and most frequent in the company of the rude. The malice there is often found in it is insinuated in the proverb, he laughs best who laughs last. It is senseless to be provoked to merriment by a mishap or a blunder, and to remain serious when we see men forgetting to live, that they may give all their time to the accumulating and hoarding of money. One may find it ridiculous too that a man should be thought superior because he lives in a great house or drives in a showy equipage, while another is contemned for the marks toil has put on him; and if the wise may ever mock and jeer, they should be allowed this privilege when they behold the servile crowd fawning on successful thieves or applauding lying demagogues.

Resignation is a virtue which religion and philosophy alike inculcate; but there is need of watchfulness lest it degenerate into indifference, sloth, negligence, and insensibility; and this danger hides also in humility, obedience, and patience — in all the passive virtues, which if cultivated overmuch beget an indolent and sluggish temper that is easily mistaken for piety. Virtue is essentially strength; and strength becomes weakness unless it exercise itself.

The stoics teach that the wise man finds his happiness, not in the things that lie without or which are subject to another's will, but within his own mind. It is objected that the disposition which makes this possible is dependent on the causes that affect health of body, and may be lost through the unbalancing of reason or the accidents which inflict such pain as to make one incapable of philosophy. This we shall admit, and yet hold that to fix one's heart on what cannot be taken from him while he remains himself is the best wisdom.

The sense of responsibility — duty, implying, as it does, moral freedom — is the deepest and holiest thing in us. It is God's witness that at the heart of all there lies, not matter and fate, but spirit and liberty. It is born of the consciousness of a Power within the soul, whose judgments are absolute, whose approval or reprobation is on all the thoughts and words and deeds of men. The supreme interests are moral. They are whatever fosters reverence and obedience, hope and courage, love and devotion; whatever lifts man above the law of physical necessity and places him in a world of freedom and joy, where if evil befall it can only be through his failure to be true to his best insight.

The Highest in the universe is a person, and the essential thing in personality is moral character.

Nothing but the self-activity of one's own mind can make him wise or good or beautiful; and hence religion and philosophy strengthen and ennoble only those whom they impel ceaselessly to think and to do.

It is a noble thing to rouse and impel to generous effort, but it is an evil and a misfortune, even though it be the effect of a great and imposing mind and character, to weaken the springs of self-activity in any human being.

To live deliberately below the truth which we know is to turn from the human self to animal impulse.

A man nobly useful is hardly to be found in ten thousand.

As well expect the unthinking to comprehend ultimate origins and ends as believe that they who live for greed or lust or ambition shall understand Christ's words when He says, Blessed are they who hunger and thirst after righteousness. The animal-minded know not nor love the things of the spirit, and are therefore unable to teach them. They may repeat formulas, but they cannot make them vital.

If there are who love me not, nor believe nor think nor feel as I, it is a result of their temperament and character; and since I cannot hope to change this, why should I be troubled?

None are persuaded against their will, and arguments fail to convince when the conclusions conflict with prejudices or interests.

The wisest and best even may not give utterance to their every thought, but to such only as they have considered, weighed, approved, and accepted. The rest are the dust and weeds of the mind.

When a new truth dawns on us our first and chief joy comes of the thought that we shall communicate it; but when we get possession of material things we feel that to share them is pain.

Labor to acquire skill in doing the things which are worth while, for to do an ill thing well doubles the fault.

As the individual advances in life, contending, striving, hoping, yearning, he gradually attains truer insight, more real knowledge, more certain wisdom; and this applies to the race as well. What is hidden from one generation dawns on another and becomes plain to the following. Were there no progress in insight and knowledge, there would be none at all.

They who have strength to bear have strength to forbear.

They who cease not to strive for the best they believe and know cannot fail.

Piety is not an end but a means to the attainment of perfect peace and joy, through perfect love.

Pity is at once sympathy and the desire to relieve. It is not natural to man more than to beasts. It is a virtue he must acquire and cultivate.

There is no worse hopelessness than to feel that one whom you love cannot be helped because he has betrayed himself and is become helpless.

They who persevere in the line of their talent accomplish much, while they who continue to do what nature never intended they should do make themselves ridiculous.

The place does not ennoble you, says Plutarch, but you exalt the place by doing what is just and generous.

No mother ever saw her son crowned with more transcendent might and glory than Napoleon's; but it hardly occurs to any one to think her either fortunate or happy. This we reserve for the mothers of men who were as good as they were great.

Principles lie deeper than interests, and they are more intimately associated with man's progress and well-being.

The rights of man are prior to the rights of property, and they are more sacred. Property is for the good of man, and to make money the primary aim, and human welfare the secondary, is a perversion of reason and conscience. The moral, domestic, and social life is more important than pecuniary profit, since the only true wealth is the life of wise and noble men and women. If material civilization dominate religious and ethical civilization, the outcome is decay and ruin.

What right hast thou to throw the burden of thy weakness and misery on another? If thou art a coward, hide thy infirmity lest it prove infectious.

If thou dost not take care of thy health no remedies will avail; if thou dost not build thy character all observances will fail.

Name and fame are worth nothing unless they make us more loving and helpful; and for others our distinctions are valuable only in so far as they become for them a source of joy, strength, and right endeavor.

They who have authority and wealth may do hurt to the noblest by their favors, but not by their injustice or neglect.

If thou art wholly in earnest and rightly employed, it will not occur to thee to ask whether others think well or ill of thee.

Since in the presence of vital truth the mass of mankind are irresponsive and lethargic, there is a kind of relief in the zeal of the unthinking, though in an age when we are deafened by their clamorous advertisements of their panaceas we may be tempted to think it would be a lesser evil if they too became comatose and voiceless.

The young are idealists, and we should foster their divine enthusiasm by helping them to believe and feel that this is God's world, where all good is stored for those who make themselves worthy, who know and love, who have faith and hope, who are true and helpful, self-active and untiring.

If thou art not moved thyself how canst thou hope to move others? The voice of the preacher is as that of one crying in the wilderness, because it is but an echo from rocks that bound the hollow waste. A phonograph would perform the function as well.

When appeal to reason is possible, appeal to memory is a mistake; for to think is a higher form of self-activity than to recall.

The facts which a learned man has information about are of small value to himself or others, unless he have a disciplined and comprehensive mind, which gives him ability to marshal and set them forth with power and in right order.

Nothing but the best mental culture gives one the power to maintain effectually the line which separates what is true from what is merely plausible.

Ideas and ideals, not less than peoples and institutions, are in ceaseless conflict, and the most vigorous and energetic, whether or not they be the truest and the highest, survive. There are no permanent facts or possessions. The celestial orbs and all that they contain are combatants on a universal battle-field where, whatever the final outcome, nothing remains unchanged.

The best reinforcement of life is found in high thoughts and generous deeds. Without them we can hardly call life human. I know an old man who by the labors and savings of years has accumulated a million dollars, but who has never cherished a noble thought nor performed an unselfish service. When I am thrown into contact with him I feel that he is and has been an unreality, the mere semblance of a man.

Whatever draws thee into solitude is a heaven-sent invitation to seek God and His kingdom within thyself. Remember this when thy friends die or forsake thee.

If we but knew how to convert all hindrances, obstacles, and discouragements into opportunities, how far might we not go toward the goal of a worthy and blessed life? There is no seeming evil, — whether it be infirm health, or the falling away of friends, or the loss of reputation or of goods, — which, if we are true to ourselves, may not be transformed into an occasion and a means of self-improvement.

When one whom we have cherished and loved drifts from us or lets us fall out of his life, he teaches us that a man's highest good and true salvation are not to be found in friendship, but in giving one's self to God.

Men are busy with their own affairs, and they will not concern themselves about thee unless they can make thee serviceable to their pleasures or interests. Hold it not a vital matter, then, whether they bear thee good or ill will.

Good deeds to be excellent must be done in a brave, cheerful, and disinterested spirit, and so wrought they are their own reward.

If thou think it worth while to remember or to dwell on thy troubles and wrongs, or thy pleasures and successes, thou art not a courageous and loving soul.

The best place is where God puts us, if there we do His will. Be not anxious about what He has reserved to Himself. What the future shall be He alone knows. Accept what is and put it to the best use. Half our misery would vanish if we refused to entertain forebodings of evils which will never befall us. Vex not thyself with thinking what thou shalt do if thy superiors or others wrong thee. Thou art not the servant of men but of God, and however thy fellows may behave toward thee, it is thy business to continue to act in all things in obedience to eternal principles.

The more thou dependest on what is outside thyself, the more slave thou art.

Mere health will often make a man contented; riches never.

They who have wrought to best purpose have been wholly intent on their work, heedless of what was or might be said of it or themselves.

If thou lovest thyself, love God; for except in, through, and for Him, what thou callest thyself is but a phantasmagory.

Love is the society of beautiful souls. However young or fair we be, our presence is not a divine boon, cannot inspire joy, hope, and courage, unless the mind be luminous and open, unless the heart be pure and generous. Love aspires — looks above, not below. It lives in worlds which the soul creates and would make eternal. Lovers wed in June because, as it is the richest and most beautiful of the months, it is the fittest symbol of the heavenly dream which exalts and beautifies them. They alone are unhappy who love not.

More than man woman must watch over her emotions, for in her more than in him sentiment tends to become folly.

Why should the wise seek the company of any one if not to learn or impart wisdom, if not to gain or give strength and joy?

In all company save in that of those we love and wholly trust we are driven to suppress what in us is best.

Let thy life-work be to create for thyself such a mind and such a heart as to make it impossible for thee to think foolishly, or to speak falsely, or to act unjustly.

The deed is the test of the genuineness of the thought; for thoughts which we have not lived or earnestly striven to live are but formal.

If we were wholly pure we might walk uncontaminated through all the contagions of vice; if we were truly wise no error could mislead, no doubt deter us from the Godward path.

Virtue is never piecemeal. To have one we must have several. The truthful are brave and loyal; the chaste are loving and faithful.

All truth, religious, moral, philosophic, scientific, and æsthetic, liberates by enlarging the sphere of consciousness and increasing the power to dwell therein as beings controlled by reason.

They are wisest who are most honest.

Self-love is the radical passion, and unless it be transcended and subsumed in self-devotion, the individual remains petty, hard, and uninteresting.

If we are not obeyed it is because we know not how to command.

Turn from those who insult thee, not in anger or hatred, but from a feeling of self-respect and because thou hast no time to give to ruffians.

So long as we strive with all our hearts to rise toward God, forgiveness of even the worst injuries is easy.

Extremes are excessive, and virtue itself may be carried to a point where it merges into vice, as they who travel eastward will, if they go far enough, find their faces turned to the west.

Success lies along the line of natural gifts; and to cultivate assiduously one's talent is to make failure impossible.

To win the highest success it is necessary to turn resolutely from most of the things men crave.

The end of labor is the acquirement of leisure to give one's self to contemplation.

Chastisement that is not medicinal degrades; unless it improve, it hardens.

An age in which the love of gain is not merely greed, but ambition, is without ideals and without distinction.

If thou hast love enough, thou hast faith enough. If we could all but know and feel that God is love, that Christ is His love made manifest, that the substance of religion is love, that they who love not are more infidel than one who, though he lack faith, strives with all his heart to be of service, — if this truth could be made to live within us, we should quickly find means to end our disputes.

In the presence of irreparable loss, of hopeless failure, of impending death, what consolation is there save in religion?

Do thy work to-day and it shall be well with thee to-morrow.

If we would make progress we must struggle and toil and cease not from labor; must drain and fill the sloughs through which our sensual nature would drag us; must level the mountains which pride and conceit raise in the path of all who are forward bent. There is no advance unless we overcome both nature and ourselves. Only so can we have foretaste of God's almightiness.

Religion, which is faith and courage, hope and confidence, strength and righteousness, leads those whom it utterly possesses to power and wealth. Its success is fatal, while they who have power and wealth, but not the spiritual mind which religion alone can give, are doomed to failure and misery.

Life is short. A little more knowledge, a little more virtue is all we can hope to gain; and for this reason the little more is infinitely precious.

The transformation of the germ into the perfect plant or animal does not excite wonder, because we see it taking place everywhere; and the evolutionary hypothesis being assumed as true, could we behold a universal transformation of the lower into the higher, we should not feel surprise. The mystery of life, however, would remain unfathomable as now, except to faith.

The test of the vitality of faith is its power to inspire virile conduct.

Seek not to excuse nor to console thyself with lies. There is no refuge for cowards.

Even they who are best hedged about with circumstance and pomp are daily placed in situations in which, were the curtain withdrawn, they would appear to be ridiculous or pitiful.

Small things are most easily preserved and

handed down: a jewel or a coin will outlast an empire; and a little volume which holds great truth in narrow bounds is apt to prove more vital than huge tomes.

The promise awakens keener interest than the deed, because we live by hope. However great our achievement, when nothing more is to be expected of us the world turns away.

A pun is wit of words, whereas true wit deals with ideas.

They who appeal to appetite and pruriency are interesting only to the depraved.

Who that is able to live in the imagination, exalted by wisdom and insight, would care to have again a relish for the naïve pleasures of childhood and youth?

Were we compelled to do the things we pursue as pastimes they would soon become intolerable; but the compulsion which drives the wise and good to follow after truth and love grows the dearer the more irresistible it is felt to be.

The words true poets write are forever magnetic and phosphorescent.

Every saintly and heroic deed strikes us as a marvel, and strengthens our confidence in human nature, as miracles heighten our faith in God.

Think not of thyself at all; or if this be impossible think modestly of thyself.

Seek the wealth which the more it is communicated the more abundantly it becomes thine — the wealth there is in wisdom, courage, and love.

If reason be not unreason, there is a right and a wrong, severed each from other everlastingly. Cleave, then, with all thy might to moral good, and it is and shall be well with thee.

The best human life even is so far beneath man's highest thought and truest insight that happiness can be found only in the yearning discontent which urges and impels to heroic striving and battling for better things.

Accommodate thyself to thy lot day by day, confident it is the best for thee if thou art true.

The many count their days by the dollars they make; the better few by the increase of truth and love within themselves.

Worldlings are vulgar, and nothing high or great is to be expected of them.

Thou wouldst not deliberately praise thyself; but what else is the speaking of aught which may raise thee in the estimation of another?

To feel no impulse toward something higher than one's self is to fail to lead a human life.

Neither excuse nor accuse thyself.

Though there should be reason for thinking that to-morrow thou shalt be accused of capital crime or raised to some exalted dignity, do thy work to-day in all earnestness and composure.

Stand firm and immovable, says St. Ignatius, as an anvil when it receives blow upon blow.

They who rightly pray do right; and they who do right pray rightly.

In the eyes of all the world the prime defect is lack of money. No other is so sure to make one appear ridiculous or contemptible. The safest are they for whom a little suffices.

In controversies and contests we take sides in obedience to interests and prejudices, and then hunt for arguments to justify our position.

Beethoven, when his ears had been closed forever to all sound, continued to beat out the celestial harmonies he could never hope to hear. So all genius does its work from inner necessity, heedless of other reward than that which the divine urgency brings.

The true function of art is interpretation. It translates nature into words and forms of truth and beauty.

We can no more build a worthy life on a basis of mere physical beauty than we can dwell in comfort in a bower of roses.

A fair face easily impoverishes both mind and heart.

Beauty, says Milton, is God's handwriting, a wayside sacrament.

No life is so wearisome and disappointing as a life of pleasure.

The great writers form clusters, and they are in literature what the great constellations are in the heavens.

If thou wouldst persuade and convince, speak what thy own experience has taught thee—*ex homine* and not *ad hominem.*

Man's spiritual being rests on a foundation of faith and hope, which reason outlines and lays, while imagination rears and adorns the temple. The true home of the most matter-of-fact, even, is built by this visionary power which weaves the vesture that makes life fair and delightful, which drapes, shields, and comforts us in youth and in age, in poverty and in riches, in sickness and in health.

The best are urged irresistibly to improve themselves; and since they feel that their environment, physical and spiritual, is part of themselves, they are urged to ceaseless labors to promote the general welfare, though they are aware all the while that no possible advance can make this earthly existence satisfactory to immortal souls.

We are charmed by a fair face and form,

until catching the utterance of the life within, we turn away like one on whom a trick has been played. Speak, says Ben Jonson, that I may see thee.

To be able to take delight in the genius, goodness, and power of another is the rarest virtue: it is the fruit of noble nature and best culture.

Ask me for anything you please, says Napoleon, except time.

If thou wouldst have strength and joy, learn to be indifferent to everything except to that which constitutes the essential good of life.

The love of God gives being to everything. Love Him and thou shalt not complain of aught.

Accustom thyself to the thought that thy rights are of minor importance, the fulfilment of thy duties being the essential thing.

The knowledge and love of truth, goodness, and beauty, which are God's being, is life at its best. Whatever helps to this, whether it be pleasure or pain, success or failure, is to be welcomed and cherished.

The sense of inner freedom which is born of the consciousness of earnest striving to upbuild one's being and to fulfil righteousness is the one unfailing source of self-respect.

Foes are the friends of the educable. They

help them to become vigilant, patient, circumspect, humble, and courageous.

My heart is more strengthened by the good I have seen in children and in the poor than by the genius of philosophers and poets.

Religion and virtue are found in the rich and in the poor; but in the poor they are more spontaneous and loving, rising without too great difficulty to higher and higher potencies, while in the rich they seem to be delicate and to require special care and nurture.

Let thy busiest and most fruitful moments be those in which thou hast nothing to do, for they who are never less idle than when seemingly idle utter the words and do the deeds which are a possession for all time.

As we open doors and windows to the rising sun and close them when it sets, so are we ever ready to welcome the prosperous and to turn from those who fail.

Be thy progress from faith to knowledge, from knowledge to wisdom, from wisdom to love.

Sound compels us more than reason. Words — the quality of voice, the tone in which they are uttered — move us more strongly than argument.

The love of money is the root of evil; but in it there is this goodness, that it is the most universal and potent stimulus to industry, without which nothing worth while can be accomplished.

Whether health or beauty or wealth be a good or an evil for thee depends on what thou art.

Chance is but a word for our ignorance of the causes by which things are produced and events come to pass.

They who are long absent from their friends become for them at last as though they had ceased to live. If it be objected that absence cannot pluck love from the heart's memory, that is true also of death.

The highest service of action is to stimulate thought and love.

Only those who give themselves to contemplation grow sublime in action.

True and helpful is the love which blends with the current of all the high aims and ends of life, and becomes an added impulse to their pursuit and accomplishment.

The significance and importance of a man lie in the vital truth he sets forth and embodies, whether in deeds or in words.

The highest courage is to dare to appear to be what one is; for they who so dare must be noble, or else shameless and not to be considered.

To recognize his master in a crowd his dog

takes a sniff at the calf of his leg, and so learns about as much of him as most men know of one another.

They who admire us give us purer pleasure than they who love us, for they are less exacting.

Did we but know Thee, O God, we should be consoled for all the ills of life.

Vital truth to be known must be felt, and it can be felt only by the lowly-minded and the pure of heart.

Evil passions punish first and worst of all those who cherish them.

We are ruined by borrowing—by borrowing trouble even more than by borrowing money.

Nothing is cheap the production of which involves the ruin of human souls and bodies.

They who lose their hearts begin by losing their heads.

The stronger thou art the more thou owest; the weaker, the greater thy claim on thy fellows.

The loss of money is gain if it create a truer appreciation of how little of it we need.

We wonder most where we are most ignorant.

If thou art indifferent to praise, detraction should not disturb thee.

The more inferior those with whom we live, the greater our need of humility.

The enemies a man's virtues make him should help him to become more virtuous.

A pure and simple heart changes life's poisons to medicines.

Faith is happiness; hope is happiness; love is happiness; true religion, which is the fine flower and fruit of faith, hope, and love, is happiness; and so long as man shall crave for happiness religion shall have influence on him.

If thy faith in God is real thou shalt see Him in what gives thee pain even more than in what gives thee pleasure.

He who feels that he cannot suffer harm from any outward wrong or deprivation has the divine mind; is a citizen of an imperishable state, a dweller in worlds where what is good and fair is so forever. Whatever happen, he is safe-sheltered.

To me nothing seems so desirable as leisure — leisure to dream, to think, to meditate, to be alone with God and the soul.

If thy enemy, intending to do thee harm, has driven thee back on the inner sources of life, know that for thee he is part of God's special providence.

Right use may be made of all things, both good and evil; and they who have this wisdom possess the secret of right living.

If thou art censured, examine thy conscience; if praised, believe it flattery.

Whatever happen, continue to work. If thou find not the buried treasure, thy labor shall make the soil fertile.

When one's convictions have been wrought into deeds they become inexpugnable.

Vigorous minds have strong passions.

They who are right can afford to pardon, whether victorious or defeated.

The fire genius kindles sets the world ablaze.

Originality, Voltaire says, is judicious selection, and Newman holds it to be the power of abstracting for one's self. They are not so far apart, for judicious selection is a kind of abstraction.

Though thou fail to make others good make thyself so.

If thy happiness be founded on the opinion others have of thee thou art miserable.

Suggestive writing is the most helpful and the most pleasing, because it creates best opportunity for discovery.

If banished from the approval of men, find paradise within.

Only that for which we have long striven and suffered becomes wholly plain to us.

A true thought outweighs a fortune. The

world finds this incredible, because its realm is seemingness and lies.

Our tastes depend on what we are. Flies batten on things men find loathsome. We are akin to what attracts us.

They who have learned to live in the realms of thought turn from what is popular and therefore vulgar. The applauding crowd is a bore. There is nothing more appealing in the gospels than the touches which present the Lord and Master, who loved and served the poor and disinherited, as shrinking from the acclaiming throng.

Were every soul of the billion and a half now living to fall asleep at the same moment, nothing would be changed. The sun would send forth heat and light, the stars would keep their places, the earth would whirl onward, the mountains would lift their peaks, the oceans would roll, the rivers flow, the flowers bloom, the birds break into song; and so would it be though from the world-wide sleep there should be no awakening. As we look backward and behold our planet a molten mass on which life is impossible, so with a glance of the mind we dip into the future and see it a frozen rock from which every vestige of life has forever disappeared.

## IV.

AS it depends on ourselves whether the flowers and the starlit heavens awaken in us emotion and aspiration, so what we are determines whether great thoughts and great purposes shall illumine and strengthen us.

The solid globe of earth is not so opaque as the obtuse and indifferent.

They whose hearts are disenthralled of the love of material things are happy in their sense of inner freedom even more than in their consciousness of possessing the power to inspire and uplift.

The exception proves the rule, because to be an exception it must stand forth in opposition to what is general. If an unselfish and disinterested man be a rare man he proves that men are self-seeking.

It is hard for a rich man to be a friend, for he suspects that not himself but his gold is the magnet; it is hard for him to be a Christian, for he knows that a follower of Christ must use his wealth to make truth and love and righteousness prevail.

Women inspire men with the noblest ambitions and hinder them from accomplishing the best.

Love is content with little, and can never have enough.

The holiest purposes and deeds are known to God alone.

If thou wouldst not debase thyself, nor insult nor wrong any human being.

Language has higher potency than bread. Bread nourishes the body, language the mind. Words not only replenish but create; not only strengthen but illumine and transform.

To be incapable of friendship is to be lacking in the essentials of humanity.

Be self-sufficient, knowing that God is always with thee; yet be persuaded that the help which man can give to man is infinite when two or three or many unite and devote themselves to some good cause.

The cock of the walk, says a French writer, is generally a goose.

The love of man for woman, says Plato, is a thing common and of course, and at first has in it more of instinct and passion than of choice; but true friendship between man and man is infinite and immortal.

In the hour of distress and misery, says Landor, the eye of every mortal turns to friendship. In the hour of gladness and conviviality what is our want? It is friendship. When the heart overflows with gratitude or any other sweet and sacred sentiment, what is the word to which it would give utterance? A friend.

The company one habitually seeks and keeps reveals character, because we are largely what we make one another — loyal or false, honest or insincere, magnanimous or mean, brave or cowardly, chaste or dissolute, hard or loving, religious or impious. In this lies the good of friendship, which is possible only to noble natures. Hence too the deep and all-pervading wretchedness which flows from wedded life when the high are mated with the low, the pure and gentle with the coarse and vulgar.

The nobler one is the less is he capable of resentment.

Nothing is interesting unless it be suffused with the light of the mind.

It is easier to respect one who bores than one who amuses us.

The solitude which nourishes the soul is the solitude of the self-active. The idle and unthinking, alone or in company, are miserable and beyond the reach of help.

The critic, says Sainte-Beuve, is one who knows and teaches others how to read.

Virtues attract no notice; vices awaken curiosity.

Like crowds that stand waiting for the doors to open, we all wait in expectancy of life till death unbars the gates.

We complain that man's life is short; but were it unending it would be intolerable.

Let a generous faith and love keep thee still superior to thy knowledge; for they who succumb to erudition are weaklings and bores.

Politeness is the child of love.

There is nothing so delightful, nothing which so surely retains its charm and freshness as the conversation of one who thinks and knows how to talk.

All noble souls, all great minds are contemporaries and compatriots.

The orator's look is part of his eloquence.

The pure reason is a corrosive. It eats away truth and beauty. It dissects and analyzes till nothing remains.

Whoever has a luminous mind and a loving heart has the power to delight though he be an hundred years old.

If thou hast a soul, give it opportunity and command.

Thy health is important, but it is not a matter for the entertainment of thy friends.

From the unhappy we seek escape as from beggars who claim our pity and help.

Everything depends on the point of view. Place thyself an hundred years backward or forward, and the billion and a half of human beings who people the earth to-day become as unimportant as the leaves the frosts have killed.

The thought and industry expended in procuring more abundant and more luxurious means of living would transform the world into a kingdom of heaven if devoted to the furtherance of a more intelligent and unselfish kind of life.

An hour with God and with one's own thoughts is worth whole days of pleasant company.

The power to help still remains when the power to please has departed.

With attention, mildness, and tact one may do almost anything in the world of men.

A not unimportant service which the really great do, they render by remaining forever interesting.

They who do not care to be of help do not care to live; for they who turn away from the power and opportunity to serve neglect what gives to life its purest joy.

Pure delight in another's good is the rarest of joys.

Think of the rights of others rather than of their duties; but where thou thyself art concerned think of thy duties, not of thy rights.

None but the frivolous would rather be loved than respected.

The most general cause of failure is unwillingness or inability to make right use of leisure.

The one purpose of business is to get the money of others; hence, to take a merely business view of life is to take a selfish and non-human view.

To think of a success in the joy it gives to a friend, says D'Aurevilly, is to drink one's nectar from a golden cup.

Nothing is so rare as great men without great faults, and it were not rash to affirm that the only pure and innocent being who has appeared in human form and exercised a world-transforming influence is Christ the Lord and Saviour. If there be another it is some disciple and follower of Him.

The primary truths of the Christian religion are the root principles of right life.

However much we boast of the sovereignty of the people, of government of, by, and through, and for them, the people know that they can do nothing right unless they are rightly counselled, led, and governed. As by instinct they look to those who are clothed with authority for guidance and command. In a popular government more than in any other, the individuals to whom the general interests are intrusted do infinite harm when they are incompetent, careless, or corrupt.

No object of our love could give us aught but pain were we to know that within an hour it would drop out of our lives forever. Happiness, therefore, is not to be found in the enjoyment of the present moment, but in looking with hope and confidence to the future.

In doing what I feel to be the command of conscience, in the belief that I have done it thoroughly well, I gain a stronger sense of the worth and goodness of life. But my purest joy, if I be not self-deceived, springs from the contemplation of the highest truth, the divinest beauty, and the absolute good; and this, as I understand it, is communion with God.

Nor State nor Church can remain vital and vigorous unless it administer the abiding truth in the manner which the conditions of the age render applicable and life-giving.

The less one knows the more certain he is that what he knows is true.

The irresolute are necessarily unhappy, for life is effort, and therefore purpose and determination.

Man knows only infinitesimally; but he is capable of believing, hoping, and loving infinitely; and he is most godlike and heroic, not when he understands but when he is uplifted and borne onward by a living, heaven-seeking faith and love.

The great mainstays of faith and religion are enthusiasm, purity of life, and property.

Poverty weaves about us a thousand bonds. Its stern and inexorable voice is not, Thou shalt not; but, Thou canst not. If one would have leisure, or visit the fairest lands, or look on the noblest works of art, or meet famous men, or employ the highest skill, or travel in the most health-begetting regions, or have faces brighten with welcoming smiles as he approaches, poverty makes it all impossible. It is hardly surprising, therefore, that the passion for gold should overmaster us. But once we have gotten wealth, it nearly always happens that we have not only become incapable of enjoying the purest delights, but have grown insensible even to the cheap pleasures which money can buy.

Compulsion is hated of all the world. The deepest in us protests against it, and bears authentic witness that consciousness of the will's freedom is primary and fundamental.

Whatever be the method and equipment, the teacher's success depends on the amount and quality of life, of love, and of earnestness which he brings to the fulfilment of his task. If he himself be apathetic, careless, and incapable, though the school building be a palace of art and science, no effective education can be given.

We hold no man who has died in a worthy cause, however terrible the manner of his death, to have been either unfortunate or unhappy. Nay, we believe his lot blessed, and are certain that he has made the best use of life in sacrificing it on the altar of what is permanently right, true, and holy; for in our inmost souls we know and feel that the highest human good is an unselfish, devoted, and heroic spirit.

Men who have played a great part have rarely disclosed the inmost motives by which their course was determined. Nothing, indeed, is more difficult than to give a true and adequate account of the influences which have controlled one's actions, even in the minor affairs of life. Our motives are as complex and as hard to unravel as human nature itself.

Give me, says Plato, beauty in the inward soul, and may the inner and the outer man be one.

Learn to feel as thy own all the good of thy fellow-men, all the joy, success, and power in which they are blameless, and thy life shall be filled with gladness and thy soul with joy.

The world-wide scandal—atheism enacted—lies in the contradiction which exists and has always existed between profession and practice — saying one thing and doing another.

When one is at college, however unpleasant the restraint, however ungrateful the task, he is consoled and strengthened by the thought that he is gaining what will be of service in after-life; and so in whatever situation we find confidence and courage, if we feel that we are growing in wisdom and virtue.

Who here and now lives with eternal things,
Drinks peace and joy from life's perennial springs.

Think not of thyself, but of the work God has given thee to do; not of happiness, but of right-doing; not of what others shall say, but of what duty commands.

It is never safe to be conspicuous, save in the performance of good, or in the utterance of right words.

If we could but learn to withdraw ourselves from trifles and to devote our leisure to thinking and to the company of immortal minds, we should know the peace and repose which is the central feeling of all blessedness.

With those who have but opinions intercourse is unprofitable. One can neither learn from them nor teach them.

The companionship of which one never tires, which the longer it continues the more pleasant and helpful it grows, is the work one loves. It deepens and purifies the fountain-head of life and joy, and it neither wears nor wearies.

Who shall love instruction? Who shall understand words of wisdom? They alone whom experience makes wise.

A gentleman is one whose mind is luminous and whose heart is pure.

Whoever is unable to look through language into the realities it symbolizes, unable to make himself the master instead of the servant of words, lacks culture and insight.

The deepest depravity is in those who prey on men's ignorances and infirmities, who advertise themselves and live in wait for the victims of sin, error, and disease, in the hope of coining their credulity and wretchedness into dollars and cents. In hell there cannot be so revolting a spectacle.

It is difficult to exaggerate the power of brave, cheerful, happy, hopeful thoughts. They create for the soul an atmosphere wherein it breathes health, couragc, and joy.

In the degree in which individuals, in which social aggregates grow in intelligence and virtue, the less men labor and the more they work.

The teaching of morality fails to touch the heart. There is in it no inspiration, no power to renew or transform, no creative spirit, no sense of exaltation. It is only when religious faith, hope, and love shine like heavenly lights on the soul, that man's whole nature is refreshed as by the breath of God. In the great crises of individuals and of peoples it is most clearly revealed that without this help from on high human life would fail utterly.

Keep thy mind and heart fixed on what is absolutely and forever true and fair, and little by little light and love shall suffuse thy whole being.

A man's joy and strength spring from the things he habitually contemplates and desires, from the quality of his love, which is the root of all virtue and the test of human worth.

Good-will to men and peace to men of good-will — this is the heavenly message; but there is need of caution lest in becoming all things to all, one lose individuality, forfeit the power of complete self-devotion to truth, which is the sole secure and eternal foundation of love.

There is no one whose opinions and conduct are not determined and controlled by his ideas of pleasure and self-interest; and since these ideas diverge and easily become opposite, tolerance is wisdom. But when there is question of what we believe to be indispensable to human welfare, we cannot but long and strive, if we are good, to make all men partakers of the divine blessing.

All existence is what it has become. Become, if thou wouldst be; cease not to grow, if thou wouldst not fall to decay.

Strength, passion, endurance, and conviction move us more than arguments. They constitute the orator's charm and endow him with persuasiveness.

Please if thou wouldst persuade.

Were ceremony done away the race would sink to lower levels, but woman would be the greatest sufferer.

They who are conscious of their integrity and worth have no resentments.

When we look on the lowly graves of great philosophers and poets we are made aware that man's home is in invisible worlds.

We do not pity those we envy, nor hate whom we despise.

Faith and works, like the sun's light and heat, are inseparable.

The honest expression of the good-will we bear one another makes no small part of life's happiness.

We are creatures of impulse, passion, and habit, and were we wholly rational life's burden would be too heavy to be borne.

Whoever gives right utterance to truth, whether he be poet, philosopher, historian, or essayist, may publish what he has written, not doubting that it will make its way in the world.

Thou wouldst not wade through sewers. It is more defiling to dip the mind into the scandals on which gossip battens.

The strenuous life ends in drudgery.

Give heed to thyself. Hadst thou thy blood from Alexander or Cæsar, if thou art worthless thy high descent would but show to what depths thou art fallen. Though thou count thy money by tens of millions, if thou art ignorant, unjust, or impure thy riches will but minister to thy base passions or barbaric pride.

Happiness is pleasure of which one need never repent.

Where there is true piety there is a brave and cheerful spirit, a generous and loving heart.

The virtuous would seem to think that they have a privilege to make themselves disagreeable, whereas in them ill-temper is doubly a vice.

The highest rewards are bestowed by what best inspires, exalts, purifies, enlarges, and strengthens the mind.

To find ourselves in the world of matter we must refer to fixed points, — east or west, north or south, zenith or nadir, and whoever has had power so to impress multitudes that when they pray they turn to some spot consecrated by him, has founded for them a religion.

As the world of which the child is conscious changes into that the youth feels and loves, which, in turn, gives way to that of the mature; so the aspirations and hopes of a people, of mankind, are subject to the law of transformation; and as the man cannot return to live in the things of his childhood, neither can a people.

The better sort are driven back on themselves, away from the noise and strife of the crowd; for only in quietude and remoteness are pure thought and love possible. It were not rash to say that the purpose of education is to accustom us to live in our own minds and consciences.

The finest natures are the most lonely. The genius seeks the solitude where none but high spirits dwell. The saint loves only the company of God and of holy thoughts. Among animals the noblest are the most solitary. Nevertheless human qualities can be awakened and developed in society only; in other words, through companionship and the interchange of good offices. The warp and woof of our life are made by society. From it we receive language, from it religion, from it institutions and arts. Of it and in it we are born and grow and become capable of thought and love. One could never rise to intelligence and conduct in isolation, could never learn to be generous or kind or just or helpful,— in a word, could never reach man's estate. But one cannot become a man in the true sense, if he live much in the company of his fellows; for unless he often withdraw into himself he can neither know nor love the best, can be neither holy nor wise, can neither rightly live nor rightly die. The noblest keep aloof and cherish solitude, not alone because their thoughts are tyrannical and over-mastering, but because they feel that in society what they best know and most love is as the witchery of sweet music to the deaf, and as blended shadings of softest colors to the blind.

Thou art little known. The great world heeds thee not at all. In brief time not so much as the echo of a name shall remain of thee. But the great world itself is hardly more enduring than the crossings and dyings of the tribes of insects. In short while all who now inhabit the earth will have sunk into it and into oblivion. Of God thou art born; live to Him.

Brief is whatever comes to end.

They whom failure can discourage or success make self-complacent are but common men.

All educators have grave responsibilities, but the gravest have those who form the men that are to counsel, guide, and govern their fellows, not in their temporal affairs, but in the things which concern character and conduct, — the welfare of the soul, for whose hurt and loss a universe gained could not compensate.

It is to his freedom that man owes the power to improve both himself and his environment; and therefore the foes of liberty are the enemies of mankind.

Where right is identified with conformity to custom, the source of noble life runs dry, while individuals and peoples fall to decay. Custom makes weaklings and cowards, unless it be ceaselessly revitalized by a current of fresh thought and love.

Incredibly great is the power of affirmation. Whatever the whole world may agree to assert with ceaseless iteration, the world will come to believe to be true.

No great work is possible where the heart does not go with the head and the hand.

Do not love me, but be my friend.

For the good life is good; for the evil it is evil. If, then, thou love thy fellow-men, do what lies in thy power to make them virtuous.

When we have learned to desire nothing which others can give, we have entered the way of peace.

It is so impossible to satisfy man with what is sufficient, that we may say the superfluous alone is necessary.

Inspiration is given only to the ceaselessly self-active.

Death rather than dishonor is a true saying; but self-inflicted, it is dishonor.

If thou wouldst be a teacher continue to teach thyself.

Indigestible and too copious food, more even than excessive drink, destroys love, friendship, and all the peace and charm of domestic life.

Whoever is a liar, a poltroon, a thief, or a lecher, is plebeian; since a truthful, fearless, upright, and chaste spirit alone gives distinction.

Though belief in the inspiration of the Scriptures should perish, faith in the Eternal Father, in Christ as His most perfect earthly embodiment, and in the Church — as the power which more than all others has the abiding gift to nourish lowly-mindedness, purity of heart, and hunger for righteousness — will survive; for there must always be many, and of the best, whom nor sexual pleasure, nor wealth, nor high place, nor science, nor culture will strongly appeal to or satisfy; and they will look above to the Father in heaven, will strive to walk in the footsteps of His Son, and will follow and love the Church which perpetuates His teaching and which keeps His spirit alive even in those who know her not.

They who have health, wealth, and fame may still be wretched, but the loving and pure of heart are never without consolation.

Spend not thy time in striving to explain difficulties, but turn thy whole thought to God, to all truth, beauty, and goodness.

It is impossible to know why God is, since for His being there is no wherefore. He is inexplicable and unfathomable, and so are His works.

We act as we feel and as we think. Let the educator therefore bend all his strength to cultivate in his pupils the power of right thinking and right feeling.

A man is worth, says Marcus Aurelius, just so much as the things are worth about which he busies himself.

Be not curious about the business or the faults of others, but attend to thyself.

Learn many things, but concentrate thy strength on some one subject of genuine value and interest.

Good health and good books, with a taste for reading, are all that is required to make life rich and delightful.

The best education, says Plato, is that which gives the mind and the body all the force, all the beauty, all the perfection of which they are capable.

Experience is the source of knowledge, and what is communicated becomes ours only when we have wrought it into our life-experience.

They who live in the public eye are made unpopular by what they say, more surely than by what they do.

As wisdom is a defence, says the Bible, so is money a defence; but learning and wisdom excel in this, that they give life to him that possesseth them. And again — God loveth none but him that dwelleth with wisdom.

There is no rule by which we may determine the worth of an individual or of a people; for the soul of a people, like that of an individual, is infinitely complex, and its value can be rightly estimated only when the thousand circumstances by which it has been constituted and moulded are thoroughly understood and appreciated.

Give me, O God, a pure heart and true thoughts.

Even great literature but feebly utters the thoughts and emotions which God and His universe awaken. The written word is like the body, which in giving a habitation to the soul, impedes and confines. To be silently good and heroic is a nobler thing than to express thoughts and sentiments, which, however fine and true, are rarely the voice of one's deepest nature. Thought and feeling are primarily for strength and guidance, not for literary ends.

A true man is content when he is tolerated by those about him; but in the face of whatever opposition he will persevere in the way he has chosen and knows to be right.

Nature forces us to care for food and drink and shelter, but is indifferent to truth, goodness, and beauty; and when man is abandoned wholly to her sway, he does not rise above a merely animal existence.

The farther we advance in science the more clearly we perceive that without faith we should sink into impotence and despair.

Men differ in their prejudices and passions more than in their thoughts, in which, when feeling and self-interest are eliminated, they easily agree, as may be seen in their readiness to consent to truths which have no application to life.

If Cæsar and his cook have alike been absorbed into the unconscious, of what benefit is it to the one that his name is known, or what disadvantage to the other that he is wholly forgotten? Fame is as unsubstantial as our other vanities.

When I recall the many things which have annoyed and worried me, but which are now as though they had never been, my present troubles grow lighter, and I scarcely think of them at all.

Fame hovers over the brows of those who look beyond her.

Whoever imagines himself to be of special worth is unimportant.

We are not impressed by seeing another do what we can easily perform. The wonderful is that which lies beyond our reach or comprehension.

The emphatic utterance of platitudes most surely wins the applause of the crowd.

It is not easy to repent of anything that has given us truer insight.

Man is the most mutable and therefore at once the most perfectible and the most corruptible of beings.

Our pleasures shorten our lives and make them miserable.

As it is a father's glory to see himself surpassed by his sons, so whoever teaches or governs should deem it the highest privilege to gather about him and form a following of men superior to himself.

There is no new wisdom; and the best genius itself can do is to give to the old truths the freshness and charm of novelty, that they who need courage, discretion, and enlightenment may be drawn to examine and consider. When left to ourselves, we turn from the teachers of wisdom to the society of those who entice us to a frivolous and aimless existence, and this is inevitable for beings for whom it is easier to sink than to rise.

Our counsels have weight only when they express what we have meditated, experienced, and habitually practised. Hence in the wisdom of the young there is an element of unreality.

Repression results in weakness, as disuse atrophies; and weakness is inferiority and servitude.

When the swiftly flying years have stolen our strength and our friends, that which still makes life's garden fair and fragrant is the memory of the smiles and the flowers we loved when the springtime of childhood and youth bloomed about us. It was then the treasure-house of our hearts was stored with the priceless gifts which we cannot lose while consciousness remains.

Gifts are precious in the degree in which they are tokens of love.

To live is to act; and if we are not busy doing good, we needs must do evil.

It is enough to know that a pure, loving, and helpful life is the only right life. Whether it be the only happy life it is not necessary to inquire.

Strive to make thyself worthy. If thou succeed thou hast the best life can give.

Nearly all we are and have we owe to our fellow-men; but to God we owe all. Our first duty, therefore, is to love and serve Him, and our second to love and serve our fellow-men.

To the youth it seems a divine, almost an impossible thing, that he should ever become a fountain-head of wisdom and strength for others; but the foreboding, however vague, of such good fortune, exalts his imagination and spurs him on to persevering effort.

The desire to please is often all that is required to make one's self agreeable.

To know where the best may be had brings it within our reach, if we are not ignoble.

There is no surer mark of mental progress than an increasing unwillingness to deny; for, as knowledge grows, the boundaries of the unknown are seen to widen. The wise, therefore, while they affirm that of which they are certain, are silent where the less enlightened are clamorous with assertion.

Without sacrifice noble life is impossible — the sacrifice of vulgar desires and easy ways, that what is difficult and higher may be attained. But all sacrifice is meaningless if the beginning and the end is blank unconsciousness. One may possibly hold that there is no truth, but who believes in truth must believe in God.

They who in every circumstance of doubt or temptation ask themselves what the Saviour would bid, and hearken to the divine voice, become not only wise and happy, but holy and blessed.

In the midst of rich pastures and the pleasant

air the animal is content; but for man faith and thought, hope and love must spring, or a paradise would become a waste. If he himself be ignoble no circumstance can redeem him from wretchedness.

The most fortunate are they who most completely upbuild their being to the full measure of their endowments; and whatever hinders this, whether it be money or pleasure or place, or poverty or friends or wife and children, is evil.

Thoughts, desires, hopes, and longings are food or poison, breed health or disease.

Introspection leads to conceit or despondency. Have good-will; do what thou canst, and let thy inner being be moulded by ceaseless right endeavor.

Political liberty is opportunity given to slaves to free themselves from within by cleaving to truth and love.

Think of the infinitude of things possible but unaccomplished, and thou shalt find no great difference between the work of a mechanic and that of a sublime genius. It is all but a children's heaping of sand to stay the incoming tide of the great ocean. Free thyself, then, of envy and conceit.

Growth is increase in quantity, development

increase in quality of life. The means of growth are food and exercise; the means of development, use and self-activity.

The lower a being is bedded, the feebler the impulse to ascend to higher things. The animal, the ignorant, and the indolent are content, while they who live in the mind and in the conscience are self-urged to rise above themselves. It is not possible to believe that those who are immersed in the mire of degrading passions should understand their condition and remain what they are. The fool knows not his folly, nor the lecher his filthiness.

Wisdom consists in a large measure in refraining from attempting too much, and in not busying one's self with what one was not born to do.

The young will tolerate no opinions they do not accept, but would set the whole world right. When experience has made them wise they are prepared to listen to all conceivable inanities and absurdities. Oh, give me back my youth with its boundless faith in the might of a single soul that trusts itself and God, and feels the irresistible power of those who wholly believe in Him. On the surface and momentarily it may be a mistaken confidence, but it is grounded on the central heart of being.

God and the other world, says Kant, are the sole end of all our philosophical inquiries, and did not the ideas of God and the other world involve and embrace morality, they were worthless.

The ideal of civilization is the making each individual a personality. To the accomplishment of this a general spread of culture can contribute little unless it be reinforced by a vital faith and the nobler passions; for no one is a personality unless he is so without circumstance, in virtue of the eternal principles which are the foundation of right human life.

It is with opinion as with fashion — what pleases to-day will appear ridiculous to-morrow. Writers, therefore, who give expression but to the passing whim are as ephemeral as milliners. The trade is imperishable; the individuals, like insects, live for a season.

Could one know the history of mankind in all its details as God knows it, it is a question whether he should most pity and abhor, or most admire and love.

As great wealth or great prosperity corrupts individuals, so does it undermine states and churches.

An earthquake which in a moment destroys thousands of lives does not arouse indignation, because it is felt to be due to causes beyond human control. Why then, since it is not in thy power to prevent the crimes and sins which make earth a hell, shouldst thou permit thyself to be disturbed by them? Take heed rather that thou become the master of thy own passions. To do this thou must not only pray and watch, but work patiently and lovingly for the good of thy fellows.

What the many crave is in the greatest demand; and they never crave the best, not even the best of sensible things. The common man, however much he be brought into contact with the perfect, loves but the common.

Here is the whole race of man — its best representatives at the least — drawn onward and upward these many thousand years; and yet when the strongest and the most enlightened minds would look into the only permanently interesting issues of life and death, they can but hope and believe.

Art thou a mere animal born to be the slave of instinct and appetite, and not rather a child of God whom He has put in His world to be guided and governed by reason and conscience?

There is no more awful mystery than the power of sin to blunt the moral sense and deaden conscience. Our responsibility is greater than we can know, and the attitude of the frivolous toward life is irrational.

However fair, amiable, and innocent one may have been, he loses interest for us once he is dead, unless his life and thought in some way reinforce and illumine our own. The beautiful are remembered as dreams are remembered; the great wrestlers with truth and goodness stamp their impress on the world.

It is not so much to his qualities as to the way in which they are blended that a man owes his character. The balance and the temper are decisive. Character is completely formed will.

The more the individual asserts his importance the less seriously is he taken. Had conceit inflated Shakespeare he would be ridiculous, as Hugo, in spite of his genius, is often ridiculous.

Truths uttered in rhythm make a deeper and more lasting impression. The poets were the first teachers of wisdom and shall forever be the most delightful.

Religious insight is the outcome of the activity of man's entire spiritual nature, in which God is revealed at once to the mind, to the conscience, and to the heart.

They who have best insight are most highly favored. It is a privilege too to be able to express what one sees and feels, for so he becomes the benefactor of the sweetest and gentlest souls.

The end of religious and moral inquiry is not to learn what religion and virtue are, but to make one's self religious and virtuous.

## V.

THE speaker and the writer attract hearers and readers, not so much by the truth they utter as by the pleasure they give. Hence when there is simply question of success, manner is more than matter. The aim should be to say mere nothings charmingly. One may get at the secret by listening to the prattle of a bright, beautiful, and unspoilt child. How easily fair young girls give delight, though they talk sheer nonsense, and when left to themselves they talk little else. Mature and wise men are carried away by their grace and babble, and they ensnare youths as hunters hares. It is an airy and indefinable illusiveness which takes us all captive — the haze that covers mountains far away, the dreamlike colors of sunset skies, the evanescent hues of flowers that fade while they bloom.

The purest source of the pleasure a writer feels in the moments of highest inspiration lies in the consciousness of the delight he shall give.

One might think it desirable to be able quickly to forget what we have suffered. Pain, however, is nearly always a penalty imposed by ignorance and folly; and to bear the smart in mind should be a help to wisdom and virtue. We find, in fact, that the young who best remember the punishments received are the most docile. Does not the memory of the sufferings we associate with wrong-doing increase the pleasure we derive from doing right?

He who sees his work grow painfully, almost imperceptibly day by day, learns the divine wisdom there is in industry and perseverance. If the inventor must fail a thousand times before he succeed, if the discoverer must grope helplessly and unwearyingly until at last a new truth or a new world dawn upon him, how shall any one hope to do aught that is excellent, unless he have infinite patience and take infinite pains?

If thy knowledge weakens moral purpose it is false knowledge, and therefore it is false if it undermines faith in God.

Desire not to appear to be beautiful or wise or virtuous or aught that may attract admiration, but strive earnestly and ceaselessly to become all that goes to the making of a fair and noble personality.

The opinions and words of others concerning thee are no concern of thine; thy one business being so to think and do as to approve thyself to thy conscience and to God.

The greatest and noblest have been formed by adversity and failure, not by prosperity and success.

Great love can teach us all that suffering and sorrow can teach.

As a true man is helped by foes not less than by friends, so is every right cause.

To seek to stay the advance of any kind of truth is to make one's self an adversary of God and a hinderer of human welfare.

They who turn from the light of religion quickly lose sight of the rights of man.

There is in living beings no stable equilibrium. They grow or they decay, physically, mentally, morally, religiously. They rise or fall, advance or recede. Hence no one is good who is not becoming better, no one is wise whose wisdom is not increasing. Hence too the instinctive impulse which drives man to make progress in whatever he sets his heart on, whether it be getting riches or fame or power or knowledge or skill or virtue.

The ideal is Truth and Love; but in the darkness in which mortal life is shrouded that which is most needful and most precious is Faith and Love.

They alone are wise who, rising above the world of the senses, accustom themselves to live with truth, goodness, and beauty. That is what Plato means when he says, that to learn how to live one must know how to die. That is the law of progress which is a quitting of lower things that the higher may be attained, a seeking of the kingdom of God first, not doubting that they who dwell therein have whatever is needful or desirable.

I had rather be in hell, says Tauler, and have God, than in heaven without Him.

One who is acquainted with the history and philosophy of life, religion, art, and science, cannot contemplate the universe from the standpoint of the multitude; yet like them he must live by faith, hope, and love, must pursue what he can neither comprehend nor fully possess; and his worth is measured not by his knowledge, but by the faith, hope, and love which are the springs of his life.

When we recall the dead whom we have known and loved, what we think of is not the body, but the soul, — the personality and character.

The decisive consideration is not what thy

thought or deed or the sum of thy life-accomplishment is worth, but what thou thyself art in virtue of the faith, hope, and love by which thou livest.

Again and again my body has perished while I myself still live. Why then shall I not survive when finally it has lost the power to remake itself?

To think is to look within, as into a vast and unfathomable ocean, which is one's self and yet not one's self, from which silently and as by stealth forms of truth and beauty rise and float a moment, and then pass unperceived except by the most serious and attentive minds.

He alone is a true and good man who makes the formation of his character the guiding purpose of his life.

Happiness, says Epictetus, lies in ourselves, in true freedom, in the conquest of every ignoble fear, in perfect self-government, in the power of contentment and peace, and in the tranquil flow of life, even in poverty, exile, disease, and the very shadow of death.

They are beautiful on whose countenances a pure, loving, brave, and cheerful spirit has left its impress.

Title and place are attractive to the immature and vulgar. A noble mind, if he have ambition, is impelled by the love of excellence and power.

The wise understand that it is only in stooping to the little things of life and nature, and in studying them with patient industry, that the secret of the greatest is learned; and they are therefore lowly-minded, reverent, mild, and serviceable.

They whom the fear of failure can deter never do the greatest things.

Should those about us agree to think us mad it would be difficult to keep faith in one's own sanity. So feeble is reason, so little does it suffice to steady thought and control imagination, it is not surprising that we should become the victims of numbers, dollars, and votes, of the things that may be weighed and counted, holding them to be the symbols and equivalents of wisdom and virtue, of truth and love.

They who imagine that not to do what can be reckoned in currency is to do nothing are the shallowest of men. What brings wisdom and virtue has the highest value, is above all price. For the multitude, however, wisdom and virtue are hardly possible, unless their labor can be weighed against coin.

The making good use of leisure brings a twofold reward, — happiness and success. It is the secret of intellectual and moral heroes, of sages and saints.

How often I hear it said, the world heeds us not, as though it had ever heeded the wise and good! To Socrates it gave the cup of poison, and to the Blessed Saviour the cross.

They threaten who are afraid or who doubt their ability. Threaten no one, says Chilo; that is a woman's trick.

We cannot act except from moment to moment; and we cannot act wisely therefore except by doing well the thing the moment assigns.

Accustom thyself to believe that what thou canst not do justly and honorably thou canst not do at all.

It is not possible to fathom the mystery of evil; but goodness is plain even to simple minds. Love it then and rejoice with all the good, not suffering thyself to be disturbed or discouraged by the deeds of the godless.

The faithful performance of the duties thy office imposes gives thee the right to leisure for study and for the diffusion of peace and joy among those thou livest with.

The three hardest things, says Chilo, are to keep secrets, to make good use of leisure, and to be able to bear injustice.

If neither wealth nor poverty is to be desired,

so neither is great learning nor great ignorance. But if we ourselves are true and loving, the more abundant our knowledge and riches, the more beneficent and the worthier we shall become, though doubtless our lives shall be the more filled with care and labor.

The loss and pain which issue in wisdom and virtue are made gain and joy.

Obey the laws, if only to keep thyself from disgrace and trouble.

The things we most rebel against we accept without a murmur when we plainly recognize that they are near and inevitable.

So many whom I have known and loved are dead. If I survive, it is to become and do good.

Religion is not a system of thought to be acquiesced in mechanically; it is a stream of truth and love which must ceaselessly refresh and enliven the whole inner being. Received merely as a formal doctrine it produces no effect. If it is to reform and recreate, it must grow within us as a germ of divine life, which to bear the best fruit must have assiduous care and nurture.

He who knows that he is born of the Eternal cannot rest content with any temporal condition; for the fact that it must come to end makes it vain in his eyes. So one who is capable of thought and love cannot be satisfied with sensation. They who are at ease, who repose in their possessions and feel not the need of ceaseless striving to rise to higher things are miserable, for they have lost consciousness of God's presence in the soul.

The finite and the infinite, the temporal and the eternal, are inconceivably diverse, and yet they are so bound together that they constitute a unity of the One and the many, of God and man.

To the undeceived and confident mind of the youthful student, if his beliefs and opinions are shattered, nothing seems longer true or worth while; but when experience and meditation shall have given him insight, he will know that though whole worlds of beliefs and opinions fail, the essential good of life remains for those who hold to its sacred worth and divine origin and end.

Nearly everything desirable any one may attain, if he despise not the means.

Be not over-confident. A word hastily spoken, a deed thoughtlessly done, a whim lightly indulged may bring disaster. The wise are watchful.

A high aim, a worthy purpose followed faithfully to the end, is success, distinction, and blessedness, whatever one's worldly fortune.

In society one should learn behavior, sympathy, forbearance, modesty, tolerance, discretion; in solitude he should acquire insight, depth, wisdom, inwardness, independence, freedom, and peace. In society he should converse with men joyfully, bravely, uprightly; in solitude he should live with God in humility and all sincerity. Our fellows are prodigals who quickly take their leave for some far distant land. We see them but a while, and even then their thoughts wander from us. God abides and is still with us though we flee Him; nor can death hide us from His face. In solitude we may make ourselves conscious of His presence and learn to know the blessedness there is in loving Him.

They alone know the truth who, heedless of the contradictions and disputes with which the world is filled, hearken to the inner voice, intent solely on doing and loving what is eternally right and good.

To those who resent hearing truth it will cease to be spoken.

If thy friend quarrel with thee, he thinks he has good cause though it be only that he is weary of thy company.

A mere nothing will often change the whole course of life. Consent heedlessly given to what seems unimportant may engage us in ways in which we can neither stay with honor nor quit without disgrace.

Since, when there is question of the best, nor number nor quantity is to be reckoned, be content with loving truth and doing good, however few there be for whom thou art a benefactor.

Pretenders need recognition. The wholly true lean on God and are self-sufficient.

What is excellent is so, though millions of eyes, blinded by ignorance or envy or prejudice, should fail to perceive its worth.

To know and to will — that is the key which opens the door to every kind of success.

So long as we can feel that vital power flows from us, to illumine, strengthen, exalt, and lead Godward even one or two, so long are we certain that it is a blessed thing to be alive.

Equality is desirable only when men are equal in what is good, or rather in the best things, since no one can believe it well that they should be uniformly ignorant or vicious.

If thou art wise thou dost not desire that any one should imagine thy words or deeds have worth they do not possess. It can do neither thee nor another good that thou shouldst be esteemed for what thou art not, and it is certain that if thy friends knew thee as thou knowest thyself, they would love thee less or not at all.

There is no higher wisdom than to strive with all one's strength for the best, indifferent as to the result, since the striving is success and blessedness.

Not reason but a common consent is the source of nearly all our opinions, and were it not for our prejudices life would lose half its charm. Could the youth see things in the light in which they shall be revealed to him when he is old, all his deep yearning and passionate desire would fail. Whatever draws us irresistibly — our religion, our country, our friends, the hope of distinction — creates about us an atmosphere in which it is not possible to see clear. "The comfortable opinion men have of themselves," says Halifax, "keepeth up human society which would be more than half destroyed without it."

To understand that wisdom consists in minding small things one need but consider that it is possible to live only from minute to minute.

They who are not able to trust their own judgment cannot be true leaders nor inspirers of noble action.

Human life is essentially a life of thought and love, of hope and joy, of faith and imagination; and the best that the most powerful and the richest can do is to foster and increase this life in themselves and in others. It is the curse of the sensualist that he can neither rightly think nor love, neither have high faith nor divine imaginings. His mind is steeped in matter; his soul in filth. He may appear to be enviable, but he is self-condemned and outside the pale of true human life.

If happiness be the ideal, they who have unselfish purposes and moderate means have greatest reason to think it may be within their reach.

To have a purpose high or low is the indispensable condition of success. There would seem to be more hope of him whose object is evil, than of one who has no fixed aim at all.

He who aims high, says Emerson, must dread an easy home and a popular manner.

Genius emerges from the midst of a mechanical and commercial environment with the greatest difficulty; but if by some happy accident one arrive at the power of perfect expression from out such circumstance, we find him endowed with the truest insight.

A man of genius may be the most practical of men, but he will love a painting, a poem, a phrase he has made more than any deeds he may have done. When Cæsar wrote, "Veni, vidi, vici," he had a higher and more exquisite delight than when he looked on the rout of his foes.

The naïve pleasure the Greek poets took in individuals and situations the man of genius must now be able to find in pure truth. The idyls of Theocritus are charming, but they touch only the things which attract the finer sort of boys and girls.

The art of writing and the art of speaking are much the same, and when all is said, they are but the art of pleasing.

The proper recreation for one whose vocation throws him into practical affairs is the study of philosophy and letters. If he acquire a taste for this it will not only give him the purest pleasure, but it will also enable him to fulfil his routine duties with greater ease and despatch.

An assumption, as unfounded as it is common, is that education is for the young only. We shall make no real progress so long as we fail to understand that each one's first and chief business, whether he is young or old, is to educate himself. It is only through the ceaseless effort to improve that we can rightly serve God or man, and service is the universal law of true human life, the sole fountain of joy.

The unintelligence of man is more dishearteninging than his perversity. The wicked may be converted, but the senseless are beyond the reach of the best skill and devotion, — all the more incurable because they are unable to perceive their need of healing.

Of all the pleasures man may enjoy on earth, says Petrarch, the cultivation of letters is the noblest, the most lasting, the most delightful, and the most constant. It is the easiest to devote one's self to and the least troublesome to procure.

Habituation is everything. Unfortunately to what lowers and enslaves we accustom ourselves readily; to what ennobles and liberates, with difficulty or not at all.

The infinite right is plain, but we are drawn to the boundless wrong. The fundamental question is whether we shall choose the right without a thought of consequences, or prefer what is pleasant or profitable. Here we have the line which separates the children of light from the children of darkness. The mystery is that it all should seem to be so largely a thing of circumstance, of heredity, of moods and temperament. But however men may differ in their attempts to explain the difficulty, the final and supreme test is conduct, not intellectual skill. Righteousness is life, and the wages of sin is death.

That a self-conscious being should spring from a universe in which at the beginning there was no self-conscious being is inconceivable and incredible. If this were possible the law of causation would lose its meaning; reason its validity. Since the eternally self-conscious One is the origin of all, He is the end of all, and matter and mind have worth in the degree in which they serve His purpose and lead to Him.

A commonplace is a truth which puts us to shame, and which, therefore, we abhor. The critics, knowing this, treat with finest scorn the moralists and the preachers.

The greatest and most sacred words have for each one the meaning and content with which they were filled for him in childhood and at home.

A man loves to talk of himself; a woman of others. He is more egotistic; she more curious.

In the gospels the enemies of Christ are always men, while the women with whom He is brought into contact are faithful and devoted.

Truth is like light, which is white but breaks into various colors. It is these colors with their infinite shadings we see, and therefore we neither see nor think alike.

Wouldst thou live long, have the will to live, exercising thyself in unwearying and disinterested striving for truth, righteousness, and love; for shouldst thou live an hundred years, occupying thyself with lower things, thy life will not have been a human life.

Wouldst thou be worthy, let not thy mind live where thy body lives — in the trough of appetite and desire.

Let old things which are true abide, and if the new are better, let them prevail.

To whomsoever the holy dead are of no consequence, says Richter, to him the living are of none.

All are sophists when they plead for themselves or what they identify with themselves, — their vanities and prejudices, their passions and interests.

The weak and unhappy are superstitious, and superstition is therefore imperishable.

Were the lives of those we deem most fortunate completely revealed to us, we should oftener pity than envy. It is ignorance that makes us harsh and bitter toward one another.

He is wise who knows how to live with all kinds of men in every variety of circumstance and condition without giving or receiving annoyance.

The contemptuous have neither religion nor philosophy; for religion is reverent and humble, and philosophy teaches us to think modestly of ourselves and kindly of others.

Were life but chance or fate, prudence were folly.

Reasons for study are plentiful, but they who give them are not teachers unless they have the secret of appealing to the imagination and of awakening a passionate, persistent longing for exercise of mind. We do not what we understand to be right or useful, but what interest, curiosity, and desire impel us to do.

The school should be a place where the young are brought into vital sympathetic relationship with the wisest, greatest, and most delightful men and women, and this acquaintance is best brought about by the personal influence of teachers working through literature.

The rightly educated are alone ladies and gentlemen. They alone keep the best company and are at home with the noble living and the noble dead.

A chief purpose in sending children to school is to have them taught the right use of leisure; for on the use we make of the time in which we have nothing to do depends our real success or failure. By our labors we gain a livelihood and acquire a certain professional or mechanical skill, but if we are to make the mind luminous, the heart generous, the imagination noble, the work must be done in our moments of leisure. So long as the school is considered mainly a useful institution it will not only fail to educate, but it will fail to prepare its pupils to perform in a cheerful and worthy spirit the tasks by which they gain the means of living. Unless they learn to look on leisure as the most precious reward of labor, they will acquire neither knowledge nor virtue.

Be grateful, if not for the sake of thy benefactors, for thy own.

No one can have all the world for his friends, but he whose life is a masquerade will easily have the contempt and scorn of all the world.

Detraction and calumny, envy and hate, help to maintain the general moral equilibrium, but they who are guilty of these vices are miserable.

They who want the sense of humor must necessarily often be ridiculous. It is as though one lacked an eye or an ear.

To the athletes of our colleges and universities we may apply what Diogenes said of a young man who danced exceedingly well — "The better, the worse."

The mind of man, says Bacon, is cheered and refreshed more by profiting in small things than by standing at a stay in great.

Our attitude toward all things is determined by the point of view from which we regard them, as our opinion of a work of art is influenced by the setting and light in which it is placed.

Whoever appeals to men gains the noblest victory when he compels them to think.

If thou canst not be a great thinker, thou canst at least acquaint thyself with great thoughts.

Poetry is to the mind what spring showers are to growing corn, and he who has not steeped himself in poetic literature must be formal, hard, and narrow. Hence the study of the great poets has been and will be the highest inspiration to the self-activity from which alone intellectual and moral culture can ripen.

Love solitude while thou art young, for the old finding themselves in the midst of a waste which the years have made, are driven to seek refuge in company.

Wealth oppresses and saddens. We have not the courage to get rid of it, and we feel that we are hoarding it for those who care little for us, and on whom it will confer no real benefit.

We do not envy others the possession of the good for which we do not care. The many are filled with envious thoughts when they behold the few who live in splendor and luxury, in idleness and dissipation, but they are content to leave the scholar to his books, the philosopher to his contemplations, the poet to his dreams, and the saint to God. None, it may be, but scholars, philosophers, poets, and saints know that the rich who live for what money can buy are of all men the least to be envied. As we must ascend to get a view of the plain, we must rise into the higher self to understand how little wealth can do to exalt the mind or ennoble the heart.

To an ape the most attractive thing in nature is an ape.

No one believes that he shall die, for hope, which never abandons us, whispers — not yet. Our life is a thing of time, and in imagination we still lengthen the portion allotted us. Not to-day nor to-morrow nor the day after shall it end; not this year nor the following: and as age comes on apace we console ourselves with thinking of those who have passed the ninetieth or the hundredth milestone, still vigorous and alert. Yet, though we thus cling to time and long for its continuance, if we are miserable we find that it drags, and if we are happy we give no heed to its passage.

They who lose health or wealth or friends move us to pity, but we are insensible in the presence of the ignorance and misery of multitudes. What they have never had we easily persuade ourselves they have no right to possess.

Learning does not make us wise or virtuous. The most it can do is to give us a sense of security, and the feeling that we are on a level with the best.

Vices are more harmful than crimes; but we punish crime and foster the vices by which it is bred.

The inextinguishable love of life is revealed not less in the sadness which softens the pleasures of memory than in the joy which hope inspires.

The purest fountain of life flows within the souls of those who are self-active in a noble way, and when the eye has grown dim and the mind has lost its fire there is still a serene joy in remembering what we have wrought in a right spirit.

There is no blessedness on earth save in hoping, believing, and striving. Nor knowledge, nor possessions, nor honors, nor pleasures can lift the cloud or lighten the burden for those who, losing heart, cease to make effort to grow in intellectual and moral power.

Hope is the fountain-head of faith; faith, of love.

They who seek gratification in what only a depraved mind and a degraded body can offer are like the beasts that batten on carrion.

The breath is poisonous; the exudations and other excrementitious matter, the elimination of which is ceaseless and indispensable to health, are poisonous. The body is the breeding-ground and burial-ground of myriads of microbes. The vital organs are closely wrapped and concealed, and when they are uncovered we turn away in horror. Yet so incapable are we of seeing things as they are that men have always considered the human body the most beautiful of objects, and Nature's masterpiece. They have been content to be its slaves, and the more completely they have been able to gratify its whims and to minister to its appetites, the more fortunate and civilized they have held themselves to be.

The purest souls are the most capable of love.

He who throws the whole stress of his thinking, loving, and doing on the power and truth and goodness of God, walks secure, certain that not death itself can harm him. He rests on an everlasting foundation, and shall not fear though worlds be shattered. But atheism destroys magnanimity, as Bacon says, and deprives human nature of the power to exalt itself above human frailty.

Light can blind not less than darkness, and the inrush of all our new knowledge has clouded the inner view of innumerable minds.

The best books are those which give us the clearest insight into our own minds and into the heart of Nature, enabling us to see God in both.

Truths we habitually meditate become part of our spiritual being, as the food we take becomes the bone and fibre of our bodies.

The best God does for us is to give us a nature profoundly religious. They who dwell in the most perfect security are not the philosophers, but the devout believers. So long as we are concerned for anything more than for the love of our Father in heaven, we are easily troubled and made unhappy.

The best is within the reach of all who have the courage and the industry to make themselves capable of knowing and loving it. It is as accessible to peasants as to kings, to simple-minded maids as to great scholars. Riches cannot give it nor poverty take it away.

All laudation partakes of self-laudation. We extol our country, our religion, our party, our friends; whatever, in a word, we identify with ourselves. Our censure too is provoked not so much by faults and vices as by the circumstance that those to whom we attribute them are persons with whom we have no sympathy.

Even to have seen a man genuinely great is a privilege for which a well-born soul remains forever grateful. Above all price, then, is the intimate acquaintance with the wisest and the best which we may make in the books wherein they have built for their spirits everlasting dwelling places.

The shallow put their trust in the improvement of the environment. They who think understand that it profits not to gain the world, if the soul be not made luminous, loving, and pure.

The true benefactors are those who minister to the mind; for man is essentially spirit, and but incidentally matter.

It is doubtful whether any one thinks worse of a sensible man than he thinks of himself. The wise, therefore, are not disturbed when they are held in slight esteem or treated as of no importance.

Thou mayest seek thyself in all things if thou but understandest that thou canst find thyself in God alone, from whom, if thou go astray, thou forsakest the source of life and joy. The infinite mystery, O Father in heaven, is that we should be Thy children and yet be blind and without love.

A generous spirit is humiliated when he disappoints, for to disappoint is to give pain. He feels that whatsoever he attempt, his fellows have the right to the best he can do; and consequently that it is his duty ceaselessly to upbuild his being, since what he is is the measure of what he can hope to perform. Nothing is more pitiful than the condition of one who, having given great promise and awakened high expectations in his youth, sinks into intellectual and moral somnolency and impotence, becoming the semblance of one who might have been a real man.

It is as difficult as it is undesirable to isolate one's self. We cannot carry with us in our travels our material and social environment; but the spiritual atmosphere, the intellectual and moral climate to which we have accustomed ourselves, accompanies us to all places, and when we have made the world of thought and love our home, we are at home everywhere.

It is well to seek strength and light from the heroes, sages, and saints of the past, but most fortunate are they who are able to drink from the fountain of wisdom and holiness as it breaks forth and flows here and now.

All that diverts, unless it be a renewal and replenishment of the inner source of life, is dissipation and enfeeblement.

When we strive earnestly to upbuild our being that we may the better serve God and man, new access to health and strength and joy is opened to us day by day.

As we turn instinctively from all that disgusts or nauseates, so let it be our life-purpose to acquire and strengthen the habit of aversion from whatever may darken the mind, weaken the will, soil the imagination, or corrupt the heart. It is a less evil to live in the midst of physical filth than with low thoughts and degrading passions.

As one who sits in his pleasant room surrounded by what he most cherishes — books and the company of those he loves — feels a deeper sense of contentment and peace when the storm rages and the rain beats on the window-panes, so he whose home is within is not disturbed by the strife and turmoil which fill the world, but gains in the midst of the noise and conflict a more living consciousness of the blessedness of his lot.

Property is the most proper of things; and they who have it in abundance make the rules of propriety, while those who have nothing appear to be ridiculous.

Passion is all-persuasive. It subdues to its own heat and color whatever it touches. Reason fades from its consuming fire as stars before the upglowing sun. It inweaves itself with Nature's laws and silences the voice of conscience. It is the subtlest of sophists, and never lacks for argument or pretext. It evolves into a philosophy which holds self-indulgence or interest or power to be man's chief good. It proclaims itself the impulse of God, stirring within the inmost depths of man's being. It becomes a religion, and makes its own gratification the aim and end of life. It is mightiest in the mighty.

To lead a human life is to believe, to hope, to think, to admire, to love, and to act in obedience to these inner powers; and so long as this is one's life, he need not consider whether he is young or old, rich or poor, famous or unknown.

Our democratic prepossessions incline us to believe that the people know and love the best.

It is not so. The heavenly kingdom is open to all, but only the few enter therein. For the most, earth is but a feeding and a breeding ground.

If an animal is beautiful it pleases and satisfies; but the fairest human body, uninformed and unillumined by a wise, loving, and brave spirit, appears to be a vulgar and unnatural thing.

Intellectual and moral not less than physical strength is odious when it is used against us; and they who have power must be beneficent if they would escape being hated.

The irresistible power of words is not given to those who hear and read and do much, but to those who dwell within and love to be alone. When Tauler found that his preaching was greatly admired, but ineffectual, he withdrew into solitude, that he might bathe in the primal source of persuasiveness and reissue a creative soul.

## VI.

THE pleasures of which the senses are the purveyors are common and cheap. They may be had by all, and the satisfaction they give is transitory and superficial. The little company of the noblest alone understand the divine joys which spring from knowing and loving the best that may be known and loved.

As a lover, despite business and distance and obstacles of whatever kind, still lives in spirit with the beloved, so a free and self-active mind, whatever difficulties and distractions may arise, is ever accompanied by great thoughts.

In a company of men some one said: I may tell this story since there are no ladies present. No, replied Grant, but there are gentlemen here.

It is amazing how naturally we respond to noble sentiments, and how easily we yield to base impulses.

If thou wouldst be wise and helpful, if thou wouldst have peace and joy, cherish above all things simplicity and purity.

To be able to abstract is, in matters of speculation, the source of original power; in practical affairs the wellspring of wisdom is to be able to generalize. Our blunders and mistakes arise from our unwillingness to recognize that we are under the reign of law, from our desire to believe that our case is exceptional. Yes, we say, we know that this generally happens, but it will not happen to us. This is the speech of the victims of passion and folly. They who play with fire get burned; but we can do it and escape harm. They who love the danger perish in it; but this does not apply to us. They who despise small things, little by little are brought to ruin; but we need not be so particular. We make exceptions of ourselves, and the ceaseless, slow-acting laws grind us to dust.

What is the body, with its cellular structure, but the result of countless acts, not in itself alone, but in the whole series of beings from which, through incalculable lapses of time, it has descended, — acts repeated until they have become habits? Its nature is its habits. This applies to the mind as well, working in and through the body. It, too, is a synthesis of habits, inherited and acquired; and its education is carried on by processes of repetition whereby its endowments, which themselves are the outcome of habits, are developed into habits of thinking, willing, and doing. Education, then, is the employment by man of Nature's methods for upbuilding and perfecting all that lives.

The more progress we make the greater the ease and rapidity with which we are able still to advance.

From Nature we receive little more than the possibility of making men of ourselves. The rest depends on the things we accustom ourselves to think, love, and do.

There are instances of persons born without arms, who have learned to write, to paint, and to perform other operations with the feet which we commonly suppose the hands alone make feasible. What imparts this skill? Use, habit, the innumerable efforts and repetitions to which their helpless condition has driven these unfortunate beings, who thus furnish us new evidence of the almost incredible things which are possible to those who have untiring industry and patience. What use will do for hand or foot, it will perform in a far greater degree for the brain, which is an immeasurably finer instrument.

Faculty is facility, and facility is the outcome of infinite repetitions, resulting in an acquired nature which makes the thing as easy to do as it is easy for the eye to see.

We are largely what heredity and environment have made us. If we have lived among the coarse and ignorant, we are coarse and ignorant. As we learn the language of our companions, we acquire their habits. They who buy and sell grow like the things they trade in. It is difficult to meet with the wise and great-hearted, and it is more difficult to rise to planes where companionship with them becomes possible. They cannot interest the indifferent and unintelligent. The vital books may be had by any one, but not the ability to understand and love them.

The creators of literature are men in whom life's current is deep and strong, and who, had their energies been directed to other forms of activity, would have wrought with the same superior power with which they wrote.

There lie as many miseries beyond riches, says Izaak Walton, as on this side them.

It is not difficult to perceive whether the author has sailed round the whole world of intelligible things, visited all the continents and islands, and sounded all the depths the mind of man may fathom, and if we find in him this comprehensiveness of view, this penetration of thought, we read him gladly, even though we be unable to assent to much he says; for he cannot fail to suggest truths and reveal beauties, of which those who have dipped only here and there into the oceans of things that may be known, are incapable of forming a conception. It is not necessary that he have plodded through the interminable details of history and science; it is enough that he be familiar with the best, and have the revealing glance which illumines all it falls upon.

They who know best how a thing ought to be done — how, for instance, a poem or a discourse should be composed — generally fail when they attempt to execute what they teach.

One who is able to live in memory and imagination, in all the ages of which history makes record, who has seen people after people, civilization after civilization, rise and flourish, and then sink to decay and death, is not disturbed by the evils which prevail around him and slowly undermine and wear away the fabric of religion and society. He understands that when there is a general decline and weakening of faith and will, the efforts of individuals are powerless to arrest the descent to ruin and extinction. He is not, however, discouraged; for a true man does brave work in the midst of whatever conditions, since it is his nature to be active and strong, and to look to God rather than to results.

It is not possible to love the company of the despondent, the faultfinding, and the complaining, of those who, condemning themselves to a private hell, would have us hear them discourse of its torments. The brave and the wise strive to make us forget their sufferings and sorrows, even though they be unable to conceal them.

The love of the weak, like their thought, is feeble. It is selfish too. They have little to give and much to receive. Hence they flatter and cling and become desperate, that they may gain ascendency over the strong and generous, who themselves grow weak when appeal is made to their nobler nature.

Great souls have nor time nor temptation to dwell on their sorrows and wrongs.

The higher manifestations of the human spirit are so life-giving that the wisest have ever been willing to forget the faults and weaknesses of those through whom they have received the divine favors.

To be shameless in sin is to make the evil doubly heinous; for it outrages not the individual self alone, but the social body whence he draws three-fourths of his life.

By four things is the world sustained, says an Arab proverb, — by the knowledge of the wise, the justice of the great, the prayer of the good, and the valor of the brave.

The sadness which overcame Gibbon when he had put the final touches to the history on which he had labored for twenty years is felt by whoever completes a great task. It is the end of so much of life and a symbol of the end of all things, and though he should know that it will bring him fame, yet is he certain that the joy he had in the doing can never be his again. For others his work may be a source of delight, but for himself it is evermore a thing done and dead.

In the world of men what is true is so interwoven with what is false that the good who come to the power of discernment hesitate to attempt to unravel the tangle lest they do harm rather than good.

There is joy in advancing, but to remain stationary, even upon an eminence to which the eyes of all the world are drawn, is wearisome.

How almost impossible it is to believe that one whom we have known to be wise, strong, and good should be guilty of weaknesses or sins to which we ourselves have no temptation!

Language gives body to thought; style clothes it with grace, distinction, elegance, and beauty, imparts to it color, vivacity, and movement.

The best literature is the work of mature minds. The writings of the young may awaken admiration, like the feats of the young athletes, but they teach nothing.

"The greatest errors are committed," says Bacon, "and the most judgment is shown in the choice of individuals." The prosperity or the decay of states and churches depends largely on the men whom they intrust with power and authority, and the wisdom of those who govern is most manifest in the kind of men they appoint to office. He is a great man who knows men, and so far as this is possible, promotes the most capable and the most honest to positions of influence and responsibility.

The foibles and vices of the greatest bear witness to the incurable weakness of man.

The infallible mark of talent is accustomableness. We can become able in the degree in which we are habituable. They who cannot inure themselves to self-activity cannot learn to do the best work. None would be unintelligent, and for none would life be uninteresting, were it possible to make the habit of attention and reflection universal. We believe, think, and do what we have grown accustomed to believe, think, and do; and if men are to be brought to believe, think, and do right, it must be the result of processes of habituation. It cannot be accomplished by argument, however conclusive, nor by exhortation, however powerful.

One may notice a fly wearying itself for hours in trying to get through a window-pane. The thing is impossible for the poor insect, but it can never know that it is so. Of how much human aim and endeavor is not this a symbol?

Part of the good fortune of youth is its impulse to believe in disinterested love, in heroic virtue, in all generous and noble sentiments; and so long as this faith abides with us, years cannot take from us the freshness of the heart, which is the very breath of the young, their crowning joy and glory.

It is the tendency of reason to discredit and enfeeble the generous emotions which spring from the heart, the conscience, and the imagination, and hence a rationalistic spirit begets a selfish and hard temper.

Great men are emulous of the great in whatever age or country they may have lived; the small are busy with efforts to surpass their little neighbors.

Beautiful is whatever gives spiritual delight,

and nothing that ministers to sensual appetite alone is beautiful.

When we love, the very defects of those we love may but serve to endear them to us, as we may see in the love of mothers for their children.

Time drags more slowly when we watch beside sleepers. The fact that it has ceased to exist for them seems to lengthen it for us.

He who makes the great orators his habitual study will become eloquent; he who lives with the great poets will acquire the poetic mind; he who assiduously meditates the sacred scriptures will become religious and devout. Little by little we are transformed into what we identify ourselves with by long and serious application.

Brevity is pleasing because it suggests and implies variety, change of thought or scene or occupation, which is indispensable to our contentment. There is nothing, however delightful, which long continuance will not deprive of its charm. Love itself cloys, and when the happy couple have gone off on their bridal tour they quickly weary of each other, and would welcome the advent of even a disagreeable acquaintance.

If we have no enemies we begin to quarrel with our friends, so difficult is it to live in peace. To the truth of this the history of individuals, families, states, and churches bears witness. Emulation and envy never die whether we live in the company of those who love us or are surrounded by foes. Enemies are teachers and benefactors, if we are capable of improvement. They make us vigilant; they keep us alert; they increase energy, inculcate prudence, inure to endurance, strengthen courage, counsel prudence, and warn against pride and presumption. Since life is a struggle, they help us to live. As a man's friends reveal his character, so do his foes. From enemies we learn patriotism, learn the worth of friends, and they hurt us only when they overcome us by filling us with anger, hatred, and revenge.

What we have grown accustomed to seems good enough, and they who fall into ways and ruts find it natural to walk therein to the end.

The vices and infamies of men are the vices and infamies of man, and they degrade us all.

Cowards are cruel because fear is the most selfish and therefore the most heartless of passions. It makes tyrants and monsters. In the fright in which they habitually live they would protect themselves by striking all the world with terror. Whatever fills us with alarm for our own safety is apt to make us reckless of the dangers and sufferings of others. In the midst of pestilences, in the rout of armies, in shipwrecks, the victims of panic easily lose the sense of humanity. No small part of the depravity of the vicious is due to the state of dread their misdeeds beget in them. The frightened are demoralized: the man dies and the beast survives. In making men brave we make them kind and helpful.

He whom no failure can dishearten, whose belief in himself no criticism can shake, whose industry no difficulties can slacken, is foredoomed to rise above the crowd. He will succeed though the object of his desire be nothing more than money and such distinction as money confers. But if the aim and end of his longing and labor be to upbuild his being, he shall become great in himself, exalted above the level of the life the many lead, and shall shed, like a fixed star, light and joy upon thousands.

In life, as in literature, the misfortunes of the brave and the beautiful are commiserated, while the sufferings and the sorrows of the decrepit and uncouth are passed unheeded by.

The sublimest emotions from which the divinest thoughts spring cannot be embodied in fitting words while we are under the spell.

What they teach us we can rightly utter only when the fervor and the glow have died away and become a memory. Even so all holiest and highest things are first truly understood and appreciated after they have passed away.

Joy expands and exalts the imagination; sorrow deepens and purifies the heart.

Can there be anything more tragical than that one who has divine gifts should suffer himself to be condemned to servitude, and live to get money when he might have been a teacher of truth and a creator of beauty?

It happens that they whom great misfortunes or sorrows have overtaken and robbed of the possibility of joy are impelled to the service and comforting of others. Despairing of their own happiness, they find relief in devoting themselves to those for whom there is hope. So long as we are of use to some one in whom we can take interest we are not wholly wretched.

There is nothing deeper in us than the desire to live in others. It lies at the root of the craving for offspring, at the heart of genius bidding it create what shall give delight and strength to many. It is part of the universal aversion to annihilation.

They who excel are modest. They see the

infinite possible, and what they have attained seems to them a slight thing.

Ignorance makes us bold; wisdom bids us pause and consider.

The consciousness that we are not living wholly for ourselves gives courage to bear the ills of life.

If the young find more exuberant delight in life than the old, they suffer more bitter pain and disappointment; for the old, in losing something of the capacity to enjoy, lose much of the illusion which gives to the ills we are all heirs to their chief poignancy.

Who hopes fears, and who believes has misgivings; and yet the bravest and the noblest hope and believe most.

"None are happy," says Leopardi, "but they who are ignorant of truth." When we consider how few there are who care for truth, who love it as they love their passions, prejudices, and interests, it scarcely seems irrational to think that they feel that a knowledge of truth would make them miserable.

The greater part of men live from mere habit, — they run on like a stream, they tread a beaten path. They are not each day inspired and made anew by fresh thoughts and a living faith; and therefore they are shallow, unhappy, and inferior.

Though all pleasure were vanity, all possession emptiness, they nevertheless who seek God, who follow after wisdom and goodness, are the least deceived and the least ignoble.

One may feel that he has been guided and protected by a special providence in a thousand ways, and yet not be justified in thinking his life has the divine approval; for one may be preserved and favored for what is to be accomplished through him and not for what he is in himself.

He who has led a worthy and useful life has built for himself a refuge into which, when he is old, he may retire and live on the memories of the past, while they who have done nothing, or but evil, are oppressed by a sense of their nullity when it is no longer possible for them to accomplish anything.

A man's ability to detach himself from his private interests and passions, and to contemplate things from a high point of view, where what is always and everywhere right and fair reveals itself, is the surest evidence of his culture and virtue.

Opinions lose hold on the people when they cease to be accepted and advocated by able minds.

The powerful and the rich have rarely been

and can hardly be virtuous, and since it is better to be virtuous than to be powerful or rich, it is easy to understand why the lowly, the mild, and the pure in heart should be happier and more blessed than kings and great captains.

The progress of the mind consists in approaching still nearer to the ultimate elements of things and ideas, in discovering in things and ideas that are held to be simple and irreducible something ulterior and still more simple. Thus all advance is from multiplicity toward unity, from variety toward identity.

We cannot know the whole of any truth, however plain it may seem to be, for every truth is involved in all truth, and since no human mind can grasp the whole system of truth, it follows that no one can comprehend even its slightest part. Faith, therefore, enters as an element into all our knowledge and science.

It may be possible to make some approach toward seeing things as they are, but to see men as they are we may not hope more than we may hope to know ourselves.

An original author must create the taste by which he is to be appreciated. He must therefore have sufficient force of thought and imagination to attract and hold readers, until they accustom themselves to look with his eyes, to see and admire what he sees and bodies forth.

True thoughts expressed in right words are as well-set jewels on the brows of fair women.

Men actively engaged in affairs have written great books, — Xenophon, for instance, and Thucydides, and Cicero, and Dante, and Shakespeare, and Bacon, and Descartes, and Goethe.

If we keep calm and unhurried, and continue to be self-active, we shall find time to do whatever the most trying situations may demand.

He whose faith is sure, whose love is pure, whose insight is true, is not disturbed or disheartened when the course of things is against him. He can do but a man's work, and in doing this in a right spirit and with all his heart he finds peace and repose.

The wider the knowledge and the deeper the view, the more difficult it becomes to have a good conscience in the midst of a world all awry.

In the measure in which we are persuaded we are persuasive.

Speak of those with whom thou hast sympathy; of others as little as may be.

They who have done none of life's drudgery cannot receive its highest rewards.

The power to know and love pure truth and

beauty is acquired, and it is necessarily lacking in the multitude who will not or cannot take the pains by which the faculty is produced.

When we look through an anthology and examine the pages chosen from the best authors, it is disappointing to find how rarely we meet with perfect writing. In the great poets there are lines and passages which could not be improved, but nearly all our English prose is defective.

Style is the essential thing in writing. The thoughts and facts belong or may belong to any one; but the setting, the coloring, the expression are the author's. They are like the tint, fragrance, and form of the flower, constituting it a thing of beauty, apart and distinct. It is in style that the creative faculty reveals itself; it is style that makes the artist, whether he be poet or painter, musician or orator.

When intellectual light and moral energy are rightly stored in the pages of a book they are made sacramental and permanently accessible to inquiring minds and yearning souls.

Few, even among scholars, are capable of discerning and appreciating beauties of style; but in every civilized age these judges are found, however small their number, and it is they who confer immortality on the chosen band. They are the arbiters of taste, and weave the crowns which do not fade.

Style is susceptible of many qualities. It may be forcible, lofty, flexible, simple, concise, lucid, cogent, poetic, logical, harmonious, rugged, sparkling, vivacious, sublime. It may take all the moods of the mind, which are infinitely various; but in each one it tends to assume the traits of his predominant thought and mood, and hence we say that style is of the man himself.

The tongue is the chief instrument of the brain. Had man never learned to speak, he would never have learned to think, would never have organized society, would never have created the arts and sciences, would never have developed civilization. Like God, he makes all things by his word.

Simplicity and clearness are the essential qualities of style. Where they are lacking there is no style. Nothing seems easier than to write naturally and lucidly, but nothing is more difficult. It is an art which much patience and pains alone can make one master of; an art which can be retained only by persevering practice and unremitting watchfulness. What is so written must seem to have been produced without effort. It impresses the reader as so inevitable that he imagines any one who had this thought or fact to express would have clothed it in these words; but the author found them only after seeking, weighing, and choosing, often indeed failed to discover them until a favoring mood or a happy accident revealed them to him, and he could never have found them at all had he not spent years in the cultivation of his style.

The religious, moral, and political life of a people, its commerce, studies, and wars, and more possibly than all these, the number and genius of its great writers are the forces by which its language is developed and polished.

Let those who have the power to persuade their fellows to read and study the vital books devote themselves to this rather than to writing something of their own, even though it have merit; for it is more important that men should apply themselves to the existing literatures than that they should be supplied with new books.

To read to find replies to objections or arguments against opponents is to turn from the pure light. Hold to thy faith, give little heed to difficulties, study to know and love truth and to embody it in thy life and words. If thou remain steadfast and walk in this way, thou shalt rise to the higher points of view where doubts and darkness fall away.

If thou suffer thyself to be tossed about by

passions and suspicions thou shalt become a disturber and malefactor.

As an illumined mind spreads light, so a peaceful soul diffuses contentment.

If thou art busy improving thyself thou shalt not be tempted to meddle with the affairs of others, nor be disturbed when others meddle with thine.

If the sense of duty be excluded from life, the root of that which gives it meaning and worth is plucked up; and if from duty love be eliminated, there remains but a skeleton: the dry bones are all in place, but there is no beauty, no joy, no soul. Now, the love which may be wedded to duty is born of religion.

The less success satisfies, the less failure discourages thee, the greater the hope that thou shalt come to understand the infinite worth of truth and love.

Agreement is easy when there is question of things for which we do not care.

Let thy sympathy be as wide as God's, who loves all that He has made.

To be afraid to die, if religion or patriotism or friendship command, is to hold the life of sensation more precious than that of righteousness and love. Hence contempt for death whenever proper occasion offers has ever been held to be a mark of noble nature. It is this, and not the physical courage, nor the butchery and ruin, that gives value and honor to the soldier's calling.

Woman wholly chaste is everywhere safe. An impure spirit cannot breathe the air which environs her.

If men would but consider the degradation, misery, and hopelessness to which fallen women are doomed, they would keep as far away as from contagion and death.

The most complete disappointment, the most bitter disillusion befalls those who seek the good of life in the indulgence of appetite and lust. They are like the insane who know their insanity and feel that it is immedicable.

There is nothing so humiliating as to know what a controlling influence the intestines have on the thoughts and ways of men. Our whole existence centres around eating, drinking, digesting, excreting, and begetting. It is miraculous that from out such a slough immortal hopes should arise.

The feebleness of the race is due chiefly to man's incontinence, above all to the incontinence of the wedded.

If the highest man and woman, the most gentle, mild, chaste, loving, patient, and helpful is the best of all we know on earth, enlightened minds shall ever be thankful that the catholic religion has prevailed, and shall cherish the hope that its influence may continue to the end.

It is not the importance of a truth but the receptive mood and temper that give it power over us. The divinest words of the Saviour have fallen on innumerable minds in whom they have struck no light and awakened no thrill of awe.

Faith can live only in hearts whose home is above the world of success, fashion, and applause; and they who are greatly influenced by these things are never true followers of Christ. Our trust is in what we love, and what we love is like ourselves. If we are material, it is matter; if spiritual, it is God. We can nor know nor follow the meek and lowly One, if we are fascinated by the pride and pomp of the world. "How can ye believe," He asks, "if ye seek praise one of another?"

The vulgar envy the rich and the powerful; choice spirits know that only the wise and loving are to be envied.

Nothing that leaves the mind unraised can be a good for man.

Lost money or reputation or place may be regained, but time misspent cannot be made good in all eternity. Never shall it be possible for us to know or to love or to be as much as we might have known and loved and been.

As self-respect forbids the tolerance of bodily uncleanness in one's self, though it be hidden, so does it command us to turn from sensual desires and deceitful and cowardly thoughts, however deeply buried within the inmost soul.

No man is good because he is not a transgressor, but he alone who strives and loves and helps.

Teach me, O God, to desire nothing save thy will and the good of my fellow-men.

The multitude are not deeply in earnest about anything, and unless one is deeply in earnest to get, whether money or position or skill, or to acquire philosophic insight or scientific knowledge or virtue or wisdom or a spiritual mind, he is and must remain one of the multitude.

Concern thyself with the words and actions of others only when duty compels, or when thou mayst find in them a source of light and strength or be of help.

Modesty is the best evidence of good sense, as to be wise in one's own conceit is the surest mark of folly.

Lying, stealing, flattery, and dissimulation are the vices of beggars, slaves, and all base and cowardly natures, and they are therefore the most contemptible of vices.

Strive to be useful and thou shalt become good; seek wisdom and thou shalt gain knowledge; seek what is right and thou shalt find what is pleasant; learn to love and blessedness shall be thine.

When nothing has power to interrupt the course of the thoughts by which we live, — not business nor worry nor travel nor infirm health, — we possess the secret of self-improvement.

It is easy to find actors who can play the parts of fools and villains, of seducers and bullies, of drunkards and hypocrites, but one who shall take that of a philosopher, a saint, or a hero is hardly to be discovered; and so in real life one may without difficulty be shallow and worthless, base and heartless, foppish and false, but they alone who contend ceaselessly and falter not make themselves wise, generous, and true.

Defend me, O eternal Father, not from my enemies, not from poverty, sickness, and death, but from myself, from my weak will and lawless passions.

The worst fate that can befall a man is to drag minds down instead of exalting them.

If thou wouldst be remembered, do or write

what shall never cease to give joy and courage. None but helpers live.

The hearts that are most deeply stirred utter the truest and the most beautiful thoughts,— most deeply stirred by the highest and the holiest things.

Since for God there is neither past nor future, for Him whatever is to be already is. Disturb not thyself overmuch, my little man.

Cats and dogs find women to love them. Why should a man be filled with conceit if he win a woman's smile?

Were it not for the conversation they hold with the dead, how lonely the best would be; and since such intercourse may be had by all, why need any one be lonely?

It is the passion in religious and moral truth that makes it communicable, and when it is set forth as dryly as a mathematical demonstration it has nor meaning nor charm.

What worse than waste of time is there not in the endless pains taken to make the mysteries of faith plain to reason? Should we comprehend them they would cease to be mysteries and would lose their efficacy.

It is a weakness with Americans that they cannot have an opinion but they would make it the foundation of a party or a sect.

No more forever shall it be possible for me to run and leap and swim and dance and spend whole days wandering in fields and woods as erstwhile. But then the blessedness of the inner life was hidden from me, which now, as the years go by, reveals itself to me more and more as the one unfailing source of joy and blessedness, while the delights of the young I recognize to be no better than the skipping of lambs and the play of colts. For this above all, O Father in heaven, am I grateful to Thee: that the soul cannot grow old. The world of my childhood and youth is become as a garden which winter has killed, and yet Thy world is more real and pleasant than when the flowers bloomed and all the year was spring.

Ignorance of the future makes life endurable. However great the pleasures or the honors which may be in store for us, if in knowing them we should be made aware of all the circumstances preceding, accompanying, and following, we should experience a sense of disillusion. Hope would lose its charm, imagination its wings, and the motives to noble effort their spring. Were the senses stronger and more acute, sights, sounds, and smells would give only pain. Were the capacity for emotion greatly increased, the world would become a place of torture. Defects provoke qualities, and the limitations which hem the soul stir within it consciousness of its immortal origin and destiny. Had man the strength of the lion, he had never developed the mightier power of mind; were the period of the helplessness of childhood shortened, he would retrograde to barbarism or savagery; were labor not required to supply his daily wants, he would content himself with an animal existence. Could the good know what a blessed thing it is to die, they might lose the courage to live.

There is no situation which may not be made the occasion for the acquirement or exercise of a virtue, whether it be prudence or patience or humility or courage or politeness or sincerity or contentedness. When all happenings are contemplated and made use of in this spirit, the soul is filled with joy and peace. Little by little we come to feel that to live is to grow, and we welcome all that offers opportunity to increase inner strength and worth, hardly caring whether it be pleasant or disagreeable.

How can a man think himself fortunate in obtaining great wealth or office, if he give heed to the fact that the involvements and obligations are a hindrance to intellectual and moral progress? "Learn to despise exterior things," says À Kempis, "and give thyself to the interior, and thou shalt see the kingdom of God come unto thee."

Fear, like love, creates its object, and it is easy to dread most the things which will never happen.

A true man is distressed by the wrong he does more than by that he suffers.

We are impelled by a law of nature to believe the things which are necessary to our peace, and faith in God is indispensable to the tranquillity and repose which are the central feeling of all happiness.

Be like a bird that chances heedless to alight
Upon a bough too frail;
Who feels the branches bend, yet sings with all his might,
Knowing his wings won't fail.

The poet's ecstasy, the painter's vision, the orator's enthusiasm, the saint's rapture, have no higher worth than a miser's madness or a lecher's craving, if there be no Supreme Spirit who, being the source and end of all things, gives all things meaning and value.

He who falls from virtue and honor falls from the summit of earthly things, and his degradation is the most complete.

If thou hast power to destroy thy fellow-man,

so has a microbe; but to have the power and the will to save is godlike.

It is only in solitude that a man belongs wholly to himself.

Though I weary of everything else, says Petrarch, I never tire of my studies, which from day to day give me more and more delight.

There are various ways of prolonging life. None is more effectual than the right use of time.

Work is for man what wings are for the bird, — the means whereby he raises himself above the earth and makes Nature his servant.

Wouldst thou become learned? Hate thy ignorance. Wouldst thou grow wise? Hate thy folly. Wouldst thou become holy? Hate thy sin.

Death has snatched thy friend from thee; but thou art running to overtake him and soon shalt be with him again.

He who is capable of entertaining an evil design will have little scruple as to the means by which it may be carried into effect.

Nothing is interesting but life, and the things each one delights in are the test of the quality of his life. The attraction of opposites is apparent merely. Nature's law is — like seeks like. Reason craves for unity; the heart for harmony. All things proceed from the One, and are drawn to their source.

It is a paltry thing to excel one's contemporaries. They who count must enter the company of the greatest in whatever age, and be measured by the standard they have fixed. The crowd of the merely successful belong to the multitude, whom oblivion quickly swallows.

To live joyfully and free from care would seem to be happiness; but were such a life the lot of man he never would have attained wisdom and courage, sympathy and love.

If men were more compassionate, more ready to spare one another pains and labors, would not will and energy and self-trust be weakened?

Nor knowledge nor wealth nor fame can be felt to be a good unless it be shared. Consciousness is a unity in duality, and the self which springs from union and communion with what is other, is free and happy only in quitting itself to find itself in those it loves and helps.

If nothing happen to fill thee with joy, think of the evil which is absent and might have befallen.

Wouldst thou know whether thy religion is genuine, whether it is joy and love and righteousness, examine whether thy life fills others with brave and cheerful thoughts, whether it spurs them to unselfish and helpful deeds.

These are the sayings of the wise men of Greece: The majority are evil; Look to the end; Seize occasion; Haste, if thou wouldst fail; Industry is everything; Know thyself; The mean is best.

A clean body is the proper shrine of an illumined and loving soul.

Thy watch ticks thirty million times a year. How much mayest thou not hope to accomplish if thou keep diligently at work?

Be thankful for whatever keeps thee humble, for it helps to save thee from folly.

The notion that to sweep and scrub and wash and sew is a woman's work, but degrading to a man, is a prejudice inherited from savages and barbarians. Lincoln, as yet little known, accompanied his wife to Louisville and carried their infant in his arms through the streets as they went from shop to shop to make their little purchases. He was abler to bear the burden and not ashamed to do any right thing. A true man feels that all honest work is honorable to man and woman alike, and he is ready to help, whatever the task that needs doing.

There is no social state more disgraceful,

says Cicero, than that in which the wealthiest are considered the best.

Nothing is so vulgar as a sneer.

They who crawl are trampled on.

Minerva's owl begins its flight
But at the approach of gathering night,
And when the shadows longer grow
Wisdom's calm face doth fairest show.

If the mind is rich, the man is rich; if the heart is full of love, life is full of joy.

As a mighty warrior routs army after army, so a vital book makes mere waste paper of whole libraries.

We long for what is permanent, yet the beauty which never changes wearies us. Were the flowers to retain their freshness they would lose their charm. Were a fair child to remain what it is it would come to appear to be unnatural. A work of art, if it be near us day by day, ceases to delight us. The immortal minds which from our bookshelves make ceaseless appeal to us are neglected. Familiarity breeds contempt and custom makes stale. The good that is at hand we care not for, but venture life and fortune to seek that which lies afar.

Merely to know what a world of wisdom and beauty is asleep around me in my books is joy and strength, even while I leave them unvisited, as a mother is happy sitting by the cradle of her slumbering child, though forgetting him her thoughts wander far away.

They who have nothing to say have often the most irresistible impulse to speak.

A thief, says Ecclesiasticus, is better than a man that is accustomed to lie.

To give pleasure is easily within the reach of the young, the frivolous, and the rich; but only the wise and loving give joy.

Habit need not give greater strength; it is sufficient that it enable us to do the things we ought with greater ease.

After the joy which springs from right-doing, the purest and sweetest is that which is born of companionship with spirits akin to our own.

It shall never be well with thee if the consciousness of doing well is not sufficient for thy peace. "Well doing — ill report — a king's portion."

# EPICTETUS

# EPICTETUS

OF the life of Epictetus little need be said. His biography is his character, and this lies open in his books, where the fine spirit of an earnest and noble soul still breathes. He was born in Phrygia, about the middle of the first century. His mother was a slave; his father is unknown. Epictetus is not his name, but is a Greek word which denotes his servile condition. In his youth he became the property of Epaphroditus, a freedman of Nero's, who permitted him to attend the lectures of Musonius Rufus, one of the most celebrated teachers in Rome. Having acquired freedom, he began himself to give lessons; but he was soon sent into exile, together with the other philosophers, by the Emperor Domitian.

Settling at Nicopolis, in Epirus (the modern Albania), he opened a school, and continued to teach the doctrines of stoicism to the time of his death, at the age, it is supposed, of nearly a hundred years. He was feeble in body, lame, poor, and unmarried, living alone until he took an old woman into his house to care for an orphan whom he had adopted. He wrote nothing, but talked with his pupils in a familiar way of whatever concerns the conduct of life. Arrian, his favorite disciple, took notes of his conversations, not with a view to publication, but for his own use. When, however, without his knowledge, they had fallen into the hands of several, he edited them himself. Thus we owe to an accident the existence of the "Discourses," which form one of the world's vital books. The "Manual" is a collection of aphorisms taken substantially from the larger work.

Epictetus was not the founder of a new philosophy. Zeno, the originator of the Stoic system, was his master, and Zeno himself derived his fundamental principles from Antisthenes, the author of the cynic school and the friend of Socrates.

The Greeks are the creators of philosophy, and their earliest attempt at systematic thought was an effort to understand Nature. But they soon learned that it was necessary to begin from within, since to know anything man must first know himself. Thus the problem of the conduct of life forced itself upon them. This is the constant preoccupation of Socrates, who was born five hundred years before Epictetus. He taught that the good is to be sought not in outward things, nor in the indulgence of appetite, but in virtue, which for him, however, is an intellectual rather than a moral habit. His calm and rational temper led him to the belief that man always acts in accordance with his knowledge, does what insight shows him to be useful to himself. He who does evil does it from a mistake of judgment. Sin is error. Virtue, then, being chiefly knowledge, may be taught, and to teach it is the philosopher's life work. But Socrates moved in a circle from which there was no escape. To know the useful is virtue. But what is the useful? That which makes for virtue.

Antisthenes does not attempt to determine the meaning of the good. He simply declares that virtue is the only good, and, in his view, virtue is the intelligent conduct of life. Right life is the essential good; virtue is its own reward, and one need not look to its results. It is, in the midst of whatever vicissitudes, a sure possession. The virtuous man is independent of events, and stands secure against fate and fortune. The world is full of things he does not need; he seeks not wealth, nor fame, nor honor, nor pleasure.

Zeno, the Stoic, born in Cyprus about 340 B. C., is the heir of the Cynics. The sage, as he conceives the truly wise and virtuous man, is first of all independent of the world, since only on this condition can he be free and find happiness in himself alone; and as what is external is but little subject to human will, he must overcome the world within himself by gaining the mastery over the feelings and desires which it excites. To be self-contained and self-sufficient, to remain unmoved in the presence of good or of evil fortune, imperturbable though the universe be shattered, is the goal he must strive to reach. If he cannot defend himself against the excitations of feeling, he will at least refuse his assent, and thereby prevent them from becoming passions. His ideal is apathy, absence of emotion. The course of things may bring him pleasure and pain, but since he holds that the one is not a good, the other not an evil, he retains his equanimity. Virtue is his sole good, and the only evil is to permit passion to conquer reason. This withdrawal of the individual within himself, however it may be modified and supplemented, is an essential element in the Stoic's conception of life. Reason, from his point of view, is not only man's nature, but that of the universe, while the impulses of the senses are irrational. The soul, as part of the World-Reason, must therefore exclude from itself all excitation of feeling.

To live in harmony with Nature is to rise into a sphere where the senses cease to trouble; it is to live in communion with the cosmic power, from which all things proceed, in cheerful obedience to the eternal destiny, which, being the will of God, is the divine law. The wise man accepts this life as his first and highest duty. It is the task which Reason imposes upon him. The Stoics, however, holding that man is by nature social, require that he lead a social life. The social ideal of the sage is that of a universal ethical community, and he is indifferent to forms of government and to actually existing states. He is a citizen of the world, demands justice and sympathy for all, and refuses to recognize the division of mankind into Greeks and barbarians.

The chief stress is laid upon the worth of moral personality, upon the paramount value of the good that lies within, though the duty of co-operating with one's fellow-men for the general welfare is inculcated. The metaphysical principle is pantheistic, and involves fatalism; but the Stoics, preoccupied exclusively with moral ideas and interests, cared little for logical consistency, and stoutly asserted the freedom of the will, holding fast to liberty of choice and to the universality of causation.

Though of Greek origin, stoicism attained its highest practical significance in Rome, where its doctrines seemed to be suited to the character of the people. Those stern, self-controlled, and brave men were attracted by a system which emphasized the value of independence, courage, and imperturbability. They found in it a source of the moral enthusiasm which the pagan religions had no power to inspire. They were drawn to the society of the philosophers, received them into their houses, and became their disciples. By daily intercourse with these earnest and austere teachers, such men as Scipio and Lælius, as Brutus, Cato, and Cicero, were formed. The prestige and authority of the preachers of stoicism were heightened by the general corruption which was undermining the state, and the public calamities which were becoming more and more frequent.

The noblest souls, despairing of the cause of liberty, withdrew from politics, and sought consolation in a philosophy which taught them how to bear the ills of life and how to die. In Rome, where only what is practical was rightly appreciated, little attention was given to the metaphysical presuppositions of stoicism, and the great teachers, losing sight of the logical requirements of the system, took what seemed to them true and to the purpose wherever it was found. Indeed, contradiction and inconsistency did not repel, as we have seen, the early Stoics, and in its Roman development the philosophy became more and more eclectic.

Epictetus, Seneca, and Marcus Aurelius are the three famous names of this later school of stoicism, and they are all teachers of the conduct of life, in love with inner perfection, and comparatively heedless of mere speculation. In the midst of the general decadence and threatening collapse of the civilized world, they sought to rouse conscience; and as the pagan religion could do nothing for them, they strove to give a kind of sacredness to human wisdom. To derive profit from their works it is not necessary to understand their theories. All that is required is an open mind and a tractable heart. What is speculative disappears in the presence of the practical worth of the truths they utter. To read them aright we need an attentive and devout spirit rather than an acute and curious intellect.

Of these three teachers of the later stoicism, Epictetus is the noblest character and the greatest authority. His life is more completely in harmony with his doctrine. He rises in moral elevation to the level of his maxims and precepts. His purity equals his insight. He is the venerable sage. He is the saint of a philosophical religion, a man who from an abject condition raised himself to the worthiest dispositions of mind and heart, who in the midst of a corrupt society remained unstained and faithful, his thought fixed on the highest moral ideals, and following to the end his vocation as a preacher of righteousness — a slave, a cripple, a pauper, as his epitaph declares, but dear to the gods. He has drawn for us an ideal of the Stoic sage, in which his own character is portrayed. He accuses neither God nor man; he controls desire; he knows not anger, nor resentment, nor envy, nor pity; he fences himself with virtuous shame. He has nothing to conceal; he does not fear exile or death, for wherever and however he is there also is God. But it is not enough that he be good in and for himself. He is a messenger sent by Zeus to instruct men concerning good and evil, to point out to them that they walk in wrong ways. He must cry out: "O mortals, whither are ye hasting? Why do ye tumble about, like the blind? The good is not in the body; it is not in wealth, or power, or empire; it lies in yourselves. God has sent you one to teach you by his example. Take notice of me that I am without a country, without a house, without an estate, without a servant: I lie on the ground; have no wife, no children, no coat, but have only earth and heaven and one poor cloak. And what need I? Am I not without sorrow, without fear? Am I not free? Did I ever blame God or man? Did I ever accuse any one? Have any of you seen me look discontented?"

Epictetus is direct, plain, and earnest in his speech. His style is bare of ornament, vigorous, and incisive. He is always serious, often stern, and at times pathetic. He does not deliver finished discourses, is heedless of rhetorical ornament, and wholly intent on improving his hearers by inciting them to the love and practice of virtue. He is not so much an orator as a brave, genuine man, whose whole being vibrates in his words, which are vital and electric. They are the honest and fearless expression of what he thinks in his heart, of what he feels and lives. They are the utterance of what is deepest and permanent in man, and therefore they never lose the power to stimulate and nourish faith in the worth of a life led in obedience to the divine commands. The simple and straightforward manner in which he speaks the highest truth has made him a favorite not with scholars merely, but with all classes of readers. Whoever is persuaded that life is chiefly conduct may derive help from him. Only the learned can read Plato with profit, and the fewest of these study him, but an ordinary mind may find in Epictetus a friend and teacher, for his philosophy is of the most practical character and easily understood. Wisdom consists in knowing how to distinguish between what is our own and what is not ours. Our will, our opinions, desires, inclinations, and aversions are ours; the rest — body, possessions, honor, and reputation — is not ours. The divine law bids us hold fast to what is our own, and make no claim to what is not ours. God in endowing us with free will gives us control over what is ours, but other things He has not placed in our power. A man's business is with himself, with learning to think rightly and to will wisely. Here he is master, here he has full control. Let him give heed to this, and in other things resign himself with a cheerful heart to the guidance of the all-wise Father who rules the whole. Since we cannot determine the course of Nature, it is our duty to accept with courage and resignation whatever befalls. Is money, or friend, or wife, or child taken from us, let us remember that they never were ours; they were but lent to us, and have been returned to the owner. Shall we complain when He asks us to restore what belongs to Him? But it lies with us to have an independent soul and a victorious will, to remain imperturbable, serene, reverent, and thankful, despite disgrace and misfortune, which cannot touch our inmost being or deprive us of freedom and virtue. These are the sole good, and so long as they are ours all else is unimportant. Will that things happen as they do, and nothing shall happen contrary to thy will. But how shall I bear the wrongs which the wicked inflict? May not God choose His agents to demand of thee what He has lent? Thou art but a player to whom a rôle has been assigned. Take cheerfully whatever character is given thee, whether it be that of a beggar or that of a king. Thy sole business is to act well the part to which God has appointed thee. Think of Him as often as thou breathest, and let thy whole study and desire be to know and do His will.

For Epictetus a virtuous life is not a means, but an end. The sage does right not from the hope of prosperity and good name, not that he may have health of body and mind, not because wise behavior produces a contented and happy temper, but he does what is just, avoids what is base, without thought of reward or punishment, impelled solely by a sense of duty. He clings to virtue though virtue be his death-sentence, and though he have no expectation of a future life. He makes no sacrifice in abandoning all things for virtue, for virtue is his only good. He who wishes to please men, who desires to be known and praised even for his virtue, is not a lover of virtue, as he who loves money or pleasure or glory is not a lover of mankind. The wise man's will rolls like a wheel with steady and even motion toward the one eternal goal, to which the universe also is drawn. "If there be any worth in thee, O man, learn to walk alone and to converse with thyself!"

In the "Manual" Epictetus appears as a stern, uncompromising Stoic. In the "Discourses" we find him in the midst of his friends and disciples, where he takes a more human and sympathetic tone. Here he infuses into his morality the glow of religion, which makes it vital and effective. We are not always made to feel that virtue lacks vigor, unless it be hard and repellent, that pride heightens truth, or that insolence is a mark of goodness, or that harshness is zeal, or modest assertion of opinion a compromise with error. We almost seem to hear Thrasea declare that he fears to hate even vice too much, lest perchance he come to hate his fellow-men. It is in the "Discourses" that he tells us that the true Stoic is "the father of mankind; that all men are his sons and all women his daughters. He attends to all, takes care of all. Is it from impertinence that he rebukes those he meets? He does it as a father, as a brother, as a minister of the common parent, Zeus." He does not marry, he has no children, he accepts no office, that nothing may interfere with the work which God has given him to do. He is careful of his health and appearance, lest he repel those whom he wishes to attract. Above all, he is clean of heart, for how, if he is himself guilty, shall he reprove others? He watches and labors for men, becomes purer day by day; he rules all his thoughts as the friend, as the minister of the gods, as a partner in the empire of Zeus. He has, besides, so much patience as to appear to the vulgar insensible and like a stone; "for there is this fine circumstance connected with the character of a Cynic: that he must be beaten like an ass, and yet when beaten must love those who beat him as the father, as the brother of all."

Epictetus does not reject the pantheism of the Stoics nor the polytheism of his age, but whatever his theological opinions, which seem to have been vague, he does not think of God as an indeterminate somewhat, but as a person to whom he is bound by ties of obedience, reverence, and love; and though he often speaks of the gods, the Supreme Being is never absent from his mind. He is the creator of the world and the ruler of all things. He cannot conceive that the universe should have come into existence or should continue without God. The glory and harmony of the creation fill him with devout enthusiasm. "What can I, a lame old man, do other than praise God? Were I a nightingale, I should perform the office of a nightingale; were I a swan, that of a swan; but as I am a rational being, I must praise God. This is my work, this I do, nor shall I cease from the task while life is left me. And upon you also I call to intone this hymn." With his last breath he hopes still to continue his sacred song: "Nothing but thanks to thee do I utter, because thou hast deemed me worthy to partake with thee of life's feast, to behold thy works, and to follow thy government of the world." Day and night he is mindful of the divine commands; his thoughts are raised to Heaven, and in earthly things he sees God, not as the Creator alone, but also as the Father who watches over His children and has care of even the least among them.

Epictetus takes what seems to him true and good wherever it be found. He has no respect for mere theory, and prizes only the knowledge which is brought to bear on the conduct of life. The beginning of philosophy, he says, is the turning from intellectual conceit and the recognition of one's own helplessness in the most indispensable things. To talk like a Stoic is easy; to live like one is difficult. He challenges his hearers to show him one whose life is in harmony with his principles. And yet all that is needed is the will. Will, and thou art free. From within come salvation and ruin. If the heart is set upon external things, a god cannot rescue thee. But let us forget the past, he cries, and begin anew. God has placed us in the midst of the battle of life; we have sworn to be true to Him, our king and leader, to defend at whatever cost the post He has assigned us. "I am thine. Where will'st thou that I live — in Rome, or Athens, or Thebes, or on the desert island of Gyara? Only, be mindful of me there."

Epictetus is not a Christian: he knows nothing of God's anger and mercy, of guilt and punishment, of redemption and forgiveness. In contradiction with his doctrine of providence, he holds to the old Stoic tradition which permits suicide, and in certain cases makes it a duty. He who can live content wherever God places him is ready to quit the tabernacle of the soul if the house is too full of smoke. Though not a Christian, he certainly knew something of the Christian religion. He lived in Rome as student and teacher of philosophy from the year 73 to 95, and at this time Christianity had penetrated even the higher circles of Roman society; and the charge of atheism which caused Domitian to send the philosophers into exile led him also to banish the Christians, many of whom suffered martyrdom while Epictetus was delivering his discourses at Nicopolis. He takes occasion to mention the heroism with which these Galileans, as he calls them, met death. They die without fear, he says, not from ignorance of the danger, nor from weariness of life, nor from madness, nor yet from philosophic conviction, but from habit. Galileans is not the name by which the Roman writers of this period designate the Christians. They did not call themselves Galileans, and to the Jews they were known as Nazarenes. It is probable, therefore, that Epictetus found the word in the New Testament writings, where the epithet is not infrequently applied to the followers of Jesus. Galen, who was educated in the Stoic philosophy and who lived but a short time after Epictetus, speaks of the contempt for death shown by "those men who are called Christians." He goes on to say that their doctrines are delivered in parables, which are more easily understood than abstruse arguments, and that their lives are in many respects like to that of the true philosophers. In fact, while the world view of the Stoic differs radically from the Christian, the moral teaching of the pagan philosopher and of the follower of Christ is often much the same. Both attach the highest importance to religious faith and sentiment; both hold that virtue is the chief good; both emphasize the principle of liberty, and draw from it that of free personality; both declare that man holds his earthly possessions as a steward of the divine owner, to whom he is responsible for the use he makes of them.

The early Stoics had taught in a general way that men are the children of God, but in Epictetus the doctrine is developed with a fulness which is found in no writer before the birth of Christ. He preaches with fiery zeal that all men are children of God, and that even slaves must be considered and treated as brothers. For him, as in the Gospel, every human being is one's neighbor. His ideal of the Cynic or perfect Stoic is that of a Christian apostle; his view of celibacy seems to have been taken from St. Paul. The portrait he draws of Hercules, as a conscious son of God and savior of the world, is very like the character of the divine Master as revealed in the New Testament, and unlike that of the traditional Hercules, who stands at the parting of the ways.

But Epictetus — though he certainly knew something of the Christian faith, and though his "Manual" was a favorite book of some of the early Christians, and became, with simply a change of certain words, a kind of rule for St. Nilus and the anchorets of Mount Sinai — remains a Stoic. For him God is not love, but the eternal destiny, and his enthusiasm for humanity is dominated by his resignation to fate. His religion is a philosophical piety founded on self-surrender to the inexorable laws of Nature. He is, nevertheless, one of those who have had the clearest insight into the duties of man, and his utterances have now for eighteen hundred years been a source of patience, courage, and strength to minds of widely varying opinions and beliefs. He is a genuine man, whose true image looks out upon us from the "Discourses." In reading him we lose sight of his metaphysical theories, and are mindful only of the great principles which he expresses with rare force and which underlie all right human life.

# MARCUS AURELIUS

# MARCUS AURELIUS

THE intimate thoughts of a wise and noble man concerning whatever touches the human heart most nearly are necessarily interesting, and when he who utters them has stood for years at the head of a vast and powerful empire his words receive a new significance, which is still further heightened by the fact that he writes not for the public, but simply to render to himself an account of himself. This is what we have in the "Meditations" of Marcus Aurelius, the Roman emperor, a man so modest, so sincere, so kindly, so magnanimous, that to know him is to conceive a higher opinion of the race which in him attains to such dignity and virtue. He was born at Rome in the year 121 of the Christian era, and died in 180, a few weeks before his fifty-ninth birthday. He was the nephew and adopted son of Antoninus Pius, whom from early manhood he assisted in administering public affairs. He became emperor at the age of forty, and reigned nineteen years, twelve of which he passed in Asia Minor, Syria, Greece, Egypt, and the countries on the Danube, putting down rebellion or defending the empire against the attacks of the barbarians, having at the same time to face various public misfortunes — inundations, famines, earthquakes, fires, and pestilence — which caused widespread misery and dismay. But though constantly surrounded by grave difficulties and dangers, and compelled to travel to almost every part of the empire, he not only found time to devote himself, as a wise and careful ruler, to even the minor interests and details of government, but also to occupy himself with the study of philosophy and his own improvement. It is the history of his inner life, as recorded in his journal, that has made him immortal, and placed him in the company of the few in whom the lovers of wisdom and perfection find it possible to take genuine delight. The book has small literary merit. The language is without elegance or distinction. He tells us that he had learned to abstain from rhetoric and poetry and fine writing. He studied simplicity and plainness in all things. He jots down detached thoughts, often merely gives us notes or indications, and his views are seldom profound or original. He is a Stoic, but does not develop or follow consistently any system of philosophy. He wavers and is uncertain precisely in those things in which a firm-rooted faith is most inspiring and invigorating. Running all through his "Meditations" there is an undercurrent of sadness and despondency. Is it because he is compelled to labor in a vocation for which Nature did not intend him, or is it due to the sight of the corruption and worthlessness of those by whom he was surrounded, indicating plainly to him that the fabric of Roman civilization was falling to ruin, or is it to be attributed to the fatalism which determines and controls his world-view? There was little either in the condition of society or in his own religious faith to cheer and strengthen; and yet it is impossible to live with him in his book without feeling that we are in the company of one of the best, wisest, and bravest of men, of one who, placed on the summit of power and splendor, was never for a moment blinded by the glitter and the show, but, looking steadily into the heart of things, remained simple, sincere, modest, self-controlled, and loving. We forget that he was an emperor; we care not in what style he utters himself; we are not curious about his metaphysical theories, or disposed to argue and dispute; it is enough that we are in his presence, that we hear his words of wisdom and Stoic piety, with the reverence, candor, and devoutness with which he speaks them.

He is a born teacher of morals, a born preacher of the surpassing worth of the inner life; and this natural bent was confirmed by his education, of which he has given an account in the first book of the "Meditations," where he mentions with gratitude that he was not sent to a public school, and that his tutors were men of character and learning. "To the gods," he says, "I am indebted for having good grandfathers, good parents, a good sister, good teachers, good associates, good kinsmen and friends — nearly everything good." He began his studies, as was the custom of the time, with rhetoric and poetry, but at the age of twelve he became a pupil of the Stoics, and adopted their austere practices as well as their dress, leading a life so abstemious and laborious as to injure his health, which remained delicate. Much of his youth was passed in the country, at the villa of Lorium, where, while continuing to read, he engaged in the pleasures of the chase, mingled with the vintagers, and occupied himself with athletic sports. Here, too, he enjoyed more exclusively the society and conversation of his mother, from whom, he tells us, he learned piety and beneficence, and abstinence not only from evil deeds, but even from evil thoughts, and simplicity in his way of living far removed from the habits of the rich. By her influence also he was strengthened to preserve intact the virginal flower of his youth. Nor does he forget to mention the admirable precepts given by his tutors, who taught him to love work, to deny himself, to endure misfortunes without complaint, not to deviate from his purpose, to be considerate of others, not to listen to evil speech, to be grave without affectation, and not to seek excuses for neglecting duty. Rusticus, whom he thanks for having made him acquainted with the "Discourses of Epictetus," warned him against the study of what is merely speculative or ornamental. The example of his masters made a greater impression even than their words; and what touched him most was their patience, firmness, equanimity, mildness, beneficence, uprightness, and sincerity. In these "Meditations" there is not the faintest trace of vanity. He is lowly-minded and the most modest of men. His candor and truthfulness are perfect. A lie seems to him to be an outrage upon his nature, upon the divinity that dwells in him. He strives not only to think and feel, but to love what he speaks. He is present in these thoughts, and we almost seem to have bodily sight of him as he lived and bore himself nearly eighteen hundred years ago.

The habit of recollection, of self-examination was recommended and practised by the Stoics before the time of Marcus Aurelius. "Each day," says Seneca, "we should call our soul to account. This was the custom of Sextius, who, before taking his nightly rest, invariably passed his conduct in review: Of what fault hast thou cured thyself to-day? What passion hast thou combated? In what hast thou become better?" And the philosopher goes on to tell us how each evening, when the light was taken from his room, and his wife, from respect for his pious practice, became silent, he also was accustomed to recall whatever he had done or spoken during the day, without dissimulating or omitting anything whatever; and that when he found aught blameworthy, he pardoned himself only on condition that the fault should not again be committed. All that concerns a good life was brought into this inquiry — the right use of time, the avoidance of the occasions of wrong-doing, human respect, the keeping guard over one's thoughts and words, mindfulness of the presence of God, of the certainty of death, and of the necessity of being prepared to meet it with courage and dignity. We do not know that Marcus Aurelius practised this daily and methodical examination of conscience, but he certainly habitually meditated the great moral truths, living in ideas, not in material interests; in principles, not in passions. In his youth even, as we learn from one of his letters to Fronto, he was accustomed to make extracts from the books he read, and to these little volumes, into which he had gathered the fine essence of the best writers, he doubtless often recurred. In this way he cultivated a taste for the brief and pregnant sayings of the Stoic and other philosophers, and found in them new incentives to lead a worthy life. A great thought, a winged word may have power not only to rouse the conscience and the will, but it may remain with us as a permanent stimulus to virtuous conduct. A phrase may fasten itself in the mind as though rivetted with bolts of steel, or it may insinuate itself into the current of our opinions and beliefs, and, blending with it, make the waters of life purer and sweeter. He loved thoughts of this kind, and he has written many which will continue to be a source of joy and strength as long as generous minds and hearts shall be found on earth. What he says has additional charm and power because he says it, because it is the utterance of a genuine man, the purity and nobleness of whose character cannot be called in question, the testimony which his contemporaries bore to his wisdom, magnanimity, and goodness being confirmed by the consenting voice of succeeding generations. How pleasant and invigorating it is to read considerations like these: "Such as thy habitual thoughts, such also will be the character of thy mind, for the soul is dyed by the thoughts. Dye it then with a continuous series of such thoughts as these; for instance, that where a man can live, there he can also live well. Live with the gods. Hold good to consist in the disposition to justice and the practice of it, and in this let thy desire terminate. The greatest part of what we say or do being unnecessary, if a man takes this away, he will have more leisure and less uneasiness. We ought to check in the series of our thoughts everything that is without a purpose and useless. What more dost thou want when thou hast done a man a service? Art thou not content that thou hast done something conformable to thy nature, and dost thou seek to be paid for it, just as if the eye demanded a recompense for seeing or the feet for walking? Have I done something for the general good? Well, then, I have had my reward. Let it not be in any man's power to say truly of thee that thou art not simple or that thou art not good, but let him be a liar whoever shall think anything of this kind about thee. Let men see, let them know a real man who lives according to Nature. If they cannot endure him, let them kill him. Look within. Within is the fountain of good, and it will ever bubble up if thou wilt ever dig."

Epictetus and Seneca had taught much of what is best in the "Thoughts" of Marcus Aurelius, but in his company we seem to breathe the air of a higher and serener world. He is meek and patient, affectionate and helpful. In his words there is nothing to recall the hard and haughty spirit of stoicism. He lives with his soul, but he finds the good of life in doing good. He is a worker, not a dreamer. He strives always to behave like a Roman, like a man; he never thinks of himself apart from his fellow-men. What is not useful for the swarm is not useful for the bee. His purpose is to keep himself holy, and to labor for the salvation of men, for the welfare of society. He seeks inner perfection in the midst of courts and camps, but neglects no duty which his high office imposes. In his tent, surrounded by barbarous hordes, he directs his armies, and still has time to write his tender and lofty thoughts. In these he finds the strength to bear the awful burden which is laid upon him. Each morning he reminds himself that he awakens to do a man's work. Philosophy is his mother, while the court is but a stepmother. "Return to philosophy frequently, and repose in her, through whom what thou meetest with in the court appears to thee tolerable, and thou appearest tolerable in the court." He is conscious of the temptations and dangers of his exalted position, and frequently makes them the subject of his "Meditations." "Take care that thou be not made into a Cæsar, that thou be not dyed with this dye, for such things happen. Keep thyself, then, simple, good, pure, serious, free from affectation, a friend of justice, a worshipper of the gods, kind, affectionate, strenuous in all proper acts. Strive to continue to be such as philosophy wished to make thee. Reverence the gods, and help men." He encourages himself in this noble purpose by recalling the example of Antoninus, his adoptive father — his constancy, his evenness in all things, his piety, the serenity of his countenance, his sweetness, his disregard of empty fame, and his efforts to understand things. He remembers how he bore with those who blamed him unjustly; how he did nothing in a hurry; how he refused to listen to calumnies; how he was content with little; how laborious, patient, and firm he was; how tolerant of those who opposed his opinions; how eager to learn.

Men must have a chief, as the world a ruler, the herd a leader; but this chief is not above the laws. His ideal is that "of a polity in which there is the same law for all, a polity administered with regard to equal rights and equal freedom of speech, and the idea of a kingly government which respects most of all the freedom of the governed." He abhors whatever is arbitrary or unjust, and finds nothing so odious as the character of a tyrant, which he couples with such epithets as black, bestial, animal, stupid, counterfeit, scurrilous, and fraudulent. He admires the martyrs of patriotism who have been the victims of tyrannical emperors. His knowledge of the incredible cruelties of some of his predecessors on the imperial throne seemed to drive him almost to excessive leniency. When he heard of the assassination of Avidius Cassius, who at the head of the armies of Asia had revolted, and against whom he was marching, he said he was sorry to be deprived of the pleasure of pardoning him. He does not think with the elder Stoics that to be virtuous one must be harsh and unbending. "In mildness and goodness," he says, "there is a higher quality of manliness." His constant aim is to unite benignity with firmness. He does not wish to be too severe even with himself. "It is not right that I should afflict myself, I who have never willingly given pain to any one." He has the tenderness and delicacy of soul of a noble woman. There is a large benevolence and sympathy in his judgment of men, even when they are perverse. He is ever ready to be of help; he is full of affection and clemency. The temple he built he dedicated to Goodness, a divinity hitherto unknown in Rome. "Love men," he says, "but with a genuine love." "Thou dost not yet love men with all thy heart." "It is not enough to forgive; thou must love those who do thee wrong." The only revenge he permits is to make one's self unlike the evil-doer. Correct, if thou canst, the wicked; if not, suffer them: for this, good-will has been given thee. Be like the vine, which bears its fruit and asks no reward. For the rest, to be a blessing to others is to be a friend to one's self. When there is question of doing good, one should be of those who know not what they do — a benefactor without thinking that any one is his debtor. What may be called his great precept is: Love mankind; follow God. He has no weak thoughts about his own happiness. It is well enough with him when he lives in accord with universal law, when he fulfils his duties as a child of God and a member of the whole human family. Besides, has he not a sure refuge within his own heart, where at every moment he may live with the thoughts which give peace to the soul? It is not necessary for him to seek the seashore or the mountains to avoid distractions, for it is always in his power to retire into himself, and to find there the things which induce the tranquil mind — those brief and fundamental principles which, whenever he recurs to them, make him calm and strong, and send him back free from all discontent to his appointed work. Thus he lives in intimate communion with the divinity present within him, and seeks in the contemplation of the laws of reason protection from temptation, discouragement, and weakness. His favorite virtues are justice and truth; but he is in tune with whatever makes for magnanimity, freedom, strength, and holiness of life. He cares not for fame, or wealth, or power, or pleasure. Things are largely what we think they are, and if we but understand that virtue is the only essential good, we shall not deem poverty, or ill health, or pain, or death an evil. One may be a divine man and be unknown, while they who are praised are praised, for the most part, ignorantly or by the false and the fickle. What, after all, is man? The earth is but a point, and the present in which alone we can live but a moment lost between two infinities. Fame is good when it increases the will and the power to do good, else it is naught, mere sound, and emptiness. The clapping of hands and the clapping of tongues are vanities in which none but the childish take delight. The emotion with which he touches on the favorite theme of dull and gloomy declaimers — the hollowness and evanescence of human life and grandeur — imparts a certain charm and freshness to his words: "Consider the times of Vespasian! Thou wilt see all these things — people marrying, bringing up children, sick, dying, warring, feasting, trafficking, cultivating the ground, flattering, obstinately arrogant, suspecting, plotting, wishing for somebody to die, grumbling about the present, loving, heaping up treasure, desiring to be consuls or kings. We see, then, that the life of these people no longer exists at all. Again, go to the times of Trajan. All is again the same. Their life, too, is gone." He is full of commonplaces on this and kindred subjects. He does not weary of them, but hunts for arguments and comparisons to express his sense of the worthlessness of fame, of the shortness of life, and the vanity of all things, especially of those which attract with the bait of pleasure or terrify by pain, or are noised abroad by the voices of men. What belongs to the body is a stream, and what belongs to the soul is a dream and a vapor. All pass quickly and are buried in oblivion, both they who remember and they who are remembered. As he grows older his sense of the hopeless sadness of life grows keener. He is still resigned, still obedient to the eternal laws, but he advances into ever-deepening gloom, where no ray of light falls. His health was broken, and the evils which he had worn himself out in trying to overcome were breaking forth again on every side. In the midst of his own family he was unhappy. His wife, though she has doubtless been the victim of calumny, had ceased to sympathize with him, and hated his friends. She had grown weary of his philosophy and of the society of philosophers. His austerity, his melancholy, his aversion to gayety and splendor, his grave maxims, were offensive to her pleasure-craving nature. Though he gave no heed to the malicious rumors about her, though he continued to love her as "his good and faithful spouse," he was depressed by the knowledge of her lack of heart for him. Commodus, his son and successor, was a cause of still more poignant sorrow than Faustina. He was a mere animal, without intelligence or feeling, and though but seventeen years old at the time of his father's death, he had already manifested something of the dispositions which made him later one of the most brutal tyrants by whom the world has been cursed.

The emperor has been blamed for not disinheriting him and adopting some one worthy to rule; but he had been proclaimed Cæsar while yet a boy, and by the time his evil nature had revealed itself Marcus was too infirm to take so decisive a step. In fact, it would have been necessary to murder him, for had he been left alive the military party, already disgusted with the rule of the philosophers, as shown in the revolt of Avidius, would have placed him at the head of the army, and plunged the empire into the horrors of civil war. And then what is more natural than that a father should believe that time and responsibility would correct the faults of his youthful son? Nevertheless, Commodus filled him with forebodings and increased his weight of care and pain, which already was too heavy for his declining strength. His friends are dead, the barbarians are in arms, the corruption of morals is spreading, faith in the gods has degenerated into gross superstition, the reforms which he had labored to bring about are superficial and ineffectual, the laws had been made better, but the life of the people continued to become more false and brutal, the army was losing its old-time loyalty and discipline — on all sides the signs of decadence were manifest.

In the midst of a falling world, in the presence of the northern hordes, menacing destruction and ruin, the emperor still meditates, still studies how he may fortify his soul. He does not despise death, but waits for it, content to see it come. It will deliver him from the sight of the corruption by which he is surrounded. His departure will not be from men who have the same principles as himself. "Come quick, O Death! lest perchance I, too, should forget myself." There will not be lacking those who are glad to see him go, whose lives his very presence condemns: "Let us at last breathe freely, being relieved from this schoolmaster." In dying he will go away from those for whom he strove, prayed, and cared so much, but who nevertheless wish to see him depart, hoping thereby to get some little advantage. "Why, then, should he desire to stay longer?" It is better to be dead than to live as they. Thou art in the grasp of fatal laws; be not like a pig that squeals and struggles when it is sacrificed, but accept with resignation what destiny decrees. Men are but leaves which the wind seizes and scatters on the ground. Thus weariness of life grows upon him, until he seems to be without God and without hope in the world. In fact, he had neither a philosophy nor a religion which can satisfy the human heart. He was never able to settle for himself the ultimate problems, the foundations of all ethical principles — God, immortality, and the freedom of the will. He speaks as a polytheist, or a theist, or a pantheist, according to his mood. At Athens he founded chairs of philosophy for the Platonic, Stoic, Peripatetic, and Epicurean schools, giving the same honor to the atheist as to the believer in the gods. At times he seems to doubt even that to which he holds most firmly. His grasp of speculative truth is feeble; he is strong and helpful only as a teacher of the conduct of life. Outside of this we find in him little but uncertainty and confusion. His moral principles even rest on no foundation of dogma, or, if on any, it is that of cosmic pantheism. His theology is as vague and variable as his philosophy. He has no settled convictions concerning the soul and its immortality. When our little boat comes to shore and we get out, he leaves it undecided whether it is to enter on another life or simply to lose all sensation, to cease to be. His thought moves between alternatives. "To go from among men, if there are gods, is not a thing to be afraid of, for the gods will not involve thee in evil; but if, indeed, they do not exist, or if they have no concern about human affairs, what is it to me to live in a universe devoid of gods or devoid of providence?" Then he reassures himself and declares that the gods do exist, and that they do care for human things; at least they place the avoidance of real evils in a man's power. But death and life, honor and dishonor, pain and pleasure, are neither good nor evil, and therefore they happen alike to all. God is for him the universal reason, the immutable law which governs all things. He is the whole, He is nature itself; the indwelling force which gives order and beauty to the universe. How this divinity, this inexorable fate, is to be reconciled with providence and with the freedom of the will, or to be made an object of prayer and adoration, he does not attempt to explain. "Out of the universe from the beginning everything which happens has been apportioned and spun out to thee." "Accept everything which happens, even if it seem disagreeable, because it leads to this, to the health of the universe and to the prosperity and felicity of Zeus." Here he joins theism and pantheism, but by Zeus he really means the universe, the universal substance of which the individual has but a very small portion. As this universal substance exists necessarily, from it by fatal laws the thread of each one's destiny is spun. "Whatever may happen to thee was prepared for thee from all eternity, and the implication of causes was from eternity spinning the thread of thy being." At times he seems to regard the universe as an immense animal, "one living being, having one substance and one soul." But it is perhaps wrong to insist on the theoretical views of a man who had little intellectual curiosity, and cared hardly at all for what is speculative. Still it is impossible not to recognize that he himself felt that the help which pantheism can offer the soul is ineffectual. Even a philosopher can derive small comfort from the thought that his absorption into the mass of matter is for the interest of the All, which contains nothing that is not for its advantage. For the multitude such a belief is without worth or meaning. Stoic morality is interesting chiefly on account of its influence upon men like Epictetus and Marcus Aurelius, who found in it a source of strength in the midst of the universal corruption in which Greco-Roman civilization was disappearing. It could never have become a principle of social regeneration. The fatalism on which it rests makes enthusiasm impossible. Its resignation is despondency; its indifference hopelessness. It lacks vitality and joyousness. There is in it no love of life, no belief in progress. The Stoic sage stands alone, conscious of his own virtue, in the midst of a world of liars and hypocrites. He is not angry with men; he is kind even, and glad to be of help; but, in truth, he has little sympathy with them. They are blind and perverse, an infinite number of fools, who are deprived of that which alone can make life bearable. Hence stoicism necessarily fails. It can neither interest nor influence the mass of mankind. It is dry and hard. It inspires no glad emotion, no immortal hope. It does not thrill the soul with the consciousness that Life is lord of Death, that truth and love lie at the heart of being, that whether we live or whether we die we are borne in the arms of the eternal Father, who knows and cares for each, even the least of His children. It cannot make us feel that the loving spirit of God leads us forth into the land of righteousness, that we are reborn into a kingdom of peace and joy and blessedness. It cannot give the faith which overcomes all things, and guides us through the portals of death into everlasting life. It has no words of pardon and comfort for sinners who repent. The power that was to regenerate the world was already active under the eyes of Marcus Aurelius, but was wholly misunderstood by him. He alludes to the Christian religion once only. "What a soul," he writes, "that is which is ready, if at any moment it must be separated from the body, and ready either to be extinguished, or dispersed, or to continue to exist; but so that this readiness comes from a man's own judgment, not from mere obstinacy, as with the Christians!" From his point of view the martyrs were obdurate fanatics and enemies of the empire. Of his humanity and tolerance there can be no doubt, but, unfortunately, there can be just as little doubt that he persecuted the Christians, or at the least permitted them to be persecuted. Intensely moral natures are apt to be narrow and rigid, and though several apologies for the new faith were addressed to him, he either never read them or was incapable of taking a world-view so utterly opposed to that of the Stoic philosophy. They who are placed in high stations are often the last to see the real trend of things, for the possession of power, like the possession of wealth or the indulgence of appetite, seems to impede insight; and this kind-hearted and spiritual-minded man had not a suspicion of the true nature of the teaching of Christ. It did not appeal to him as a philosophy, and as a religion it seemed to him atheistic, for it denied the existence of the gods whom he revered and whose worship he thought inseparable from loyalty to the empire. He felt, as all the thoughtful minds of the time felt, that here was a new spirit, which, if it should prevail, would lead to the overthrow of the old civilization. He may not have held with Tacitus that the Christians were convicted of hatred of the human race, but he believed that they were the enemies of the Roman state. The ancients looked upon religion as essentially a national affair. They had no conception of what we understand by liberty of conscience. The appeal from Cæsar to God was for them meaningless, if not impious. When the Christians declared that they were ready to obey all civil and military laws, but reserved to themselves freedom to worship God according to the principles of their faith, which forbade them to offer sacrifice to idols, they uttered words which their enemies could not understand, words which Christians themselves in later ages have often been unable or unwilling to understand.

It was but two or three years before the death of Marcus Aurelius that the persecution broke forth at Lyons. The emperor, who became prematurely old, was in feeble health and surrounded by dangers and difficulties. The populace, eager to believe the Christians guilty of the most atrocious crimes, attributed whatever evils befell the state to the anger of the gods against their contemners, and clamored for their punishment. The emperor yielded to the popular fury, and the church of Lyons gave to the world an example of heroism which, if ever equalled, has never been surpassed. It is the very irony of fate that Marcus Aurelius should be counted among the persecutors of the Christians, that his name should be coupled with those of Nero and Domitian. It is doubtful whether he himself issued a new edict or simply permitted those of his predecessors to be enforced. Melito, Bishop of Sardis, who addressed a letter to the emperor, leads us to suppose that he had sent forth decrees which resulted in the martyrdom of St. Polycarp, Bishop of Smyrna, ten years before the persecution at Lyons.

On the other hand, Tertullian, writing twenty years after the death of Marcus Aurelius, affirms in the most positive manner that he protected the Christians; that if he did not expressly revoke the edicts of former emperors against them, he at least rendered them ineffective by establishing penalties against their accusers. It seems probable that he was not an active persecutor; but he certainly lived and died with an utter misconception of the religion which even then was the only vital force left to a perishing world.

He was, nevertheless, one of the most just and clement of men. There is little genuine wisdom and goodness anywhere, and what there is is rarely found in the palaces of kings and emperors. Let us try to imagine a European ruler or an American President of our day who should be busy with the thoughts and aspirations of Marcus Aurelius. The mere idea seems to be grotesque. He is one in whom the wise have recognized the genuine goodness which has the mark of universality, which, like the best culture, lifts its possessor above party and country, and makes him a blessing for mankind and for all time.

In reading his "Meditations" we are always in the presence of a magnanimous man, of a great soul whose kindliness and good faith we cannot doubt unless we ourselves lack love and truth. He will remain in literature as one of its great spiritual forces. He has the vital touch which gives immortality, because it reveals a noble and interesting personality. There is in him the indefinable something which makes writing literature. It is doubtless largely sincerity, the perfect truthfulness which makes the word the mirror of the man. Much of what he says is said by Seneca and Epictetus, but in it there is an accent of his own which gives it a fresh meaning, a new quality. In these disconnected "Thoughts," in spite of repetitions, of incorrectness, and obscurity, there breathes a soul that cannot die, there stands forth a character which all men must deem it a privilege to know. The book is alive with the high and rare qualities which go to the making of a true and noble man. In the little casket found in the tent on the Danube where he died there was stored a life which death could not extinguish. The "Meditations" with which he fortified his own spirit in the struggle for better and higher life have consoled and will continue to console kindred spirits in every age; for whatever his doubts and misgivings, his faith in duty and affection, in the supreme worth of righteousness, was never shaken. His victories are forgotten; his efforts to improve the laws, to spread enlightenment, to help the orphans, are hardly remembered; but fame, for which he cared not at all, is his forever, and of our many vanities perhaps the least vain is the fame which rests on words that never lose their power to inspire, to illumine, and to strengthen. The whole earth is the sepulchre of illustrious men, but it is so only when the greatness of soul which shone forth in their lives is kept in imperishable vigor in some immortal book.